AF379162

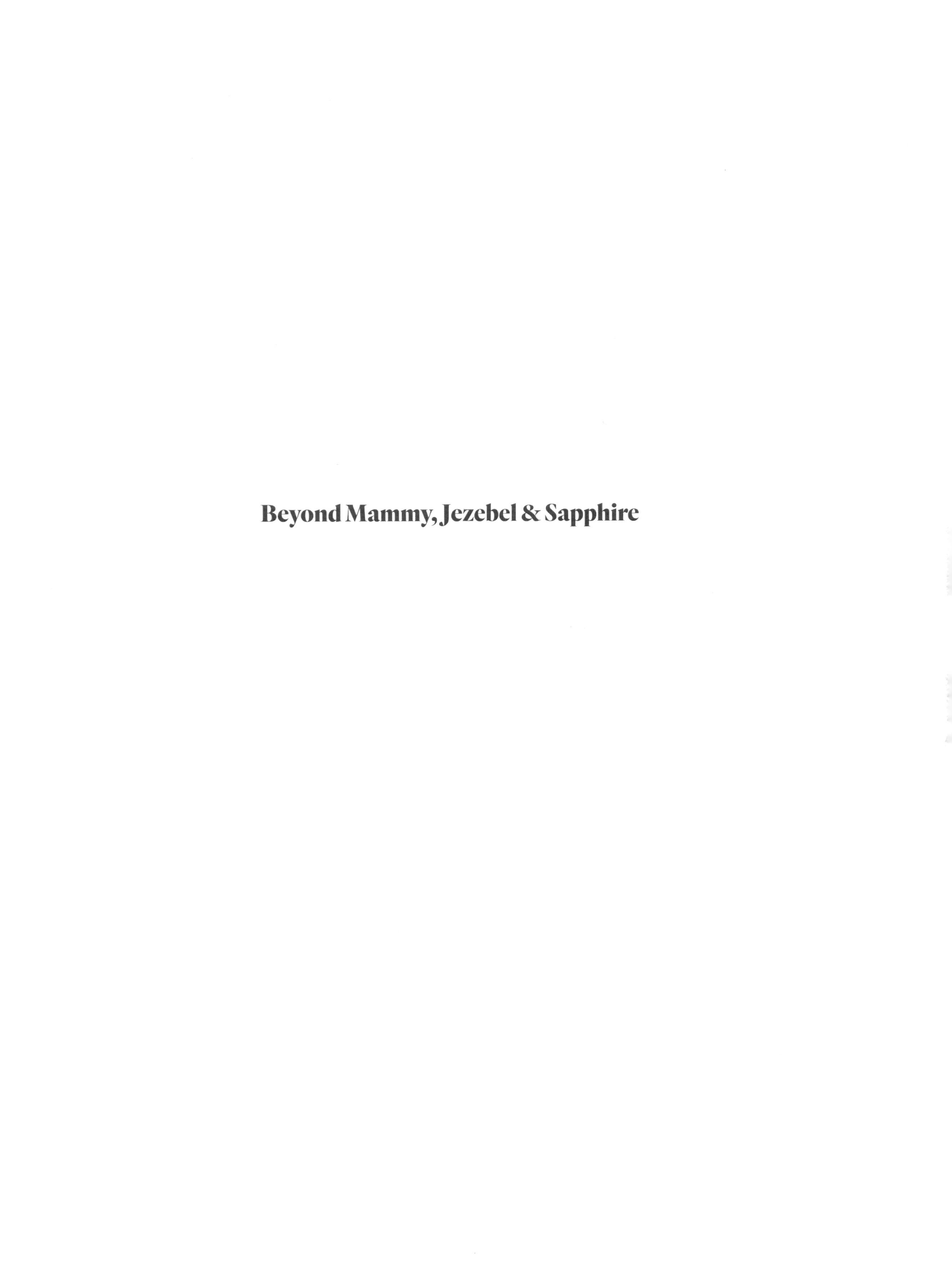

Beyond Mammy, Jezebel & Sapphire

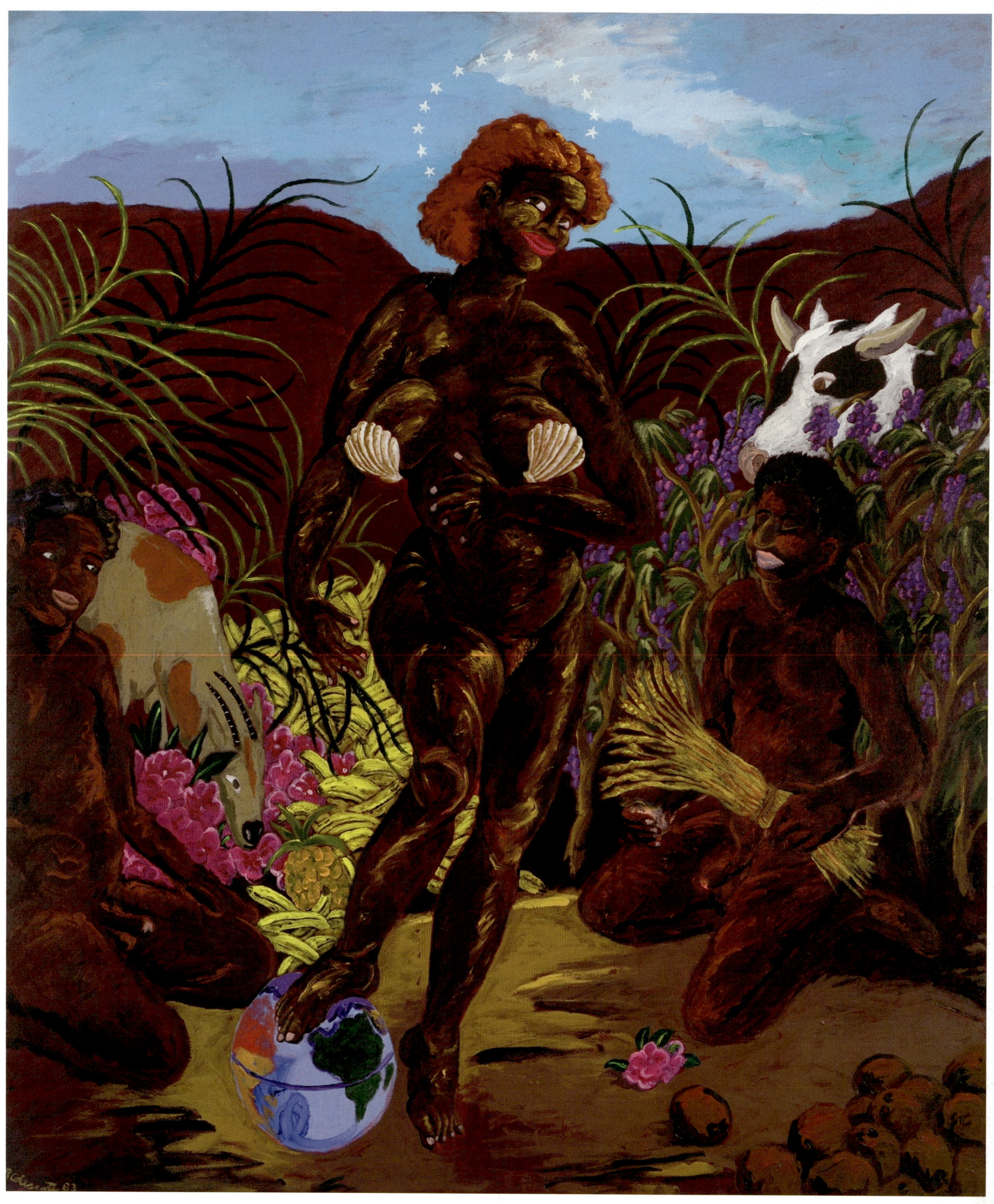

Beyond Mammy, Jezebel & Sapphire

RECLAIMING IMAGES OF BLACK WOMEN

Works from the Collections of Jordan D. Schnitzer and his Family Foundation

ESSAYS BY

Heidi R. Lewis and Roland Mitchell

CONTRIBUTIONS BY

Takiyah Nur Amin

Velva Boles

Claire Garcia

Jean Gumpper

Kate Leonard

Venetria K. Patton

Sha'Condria Sibley

Karen Riley Simmons

Claudine Taaffe

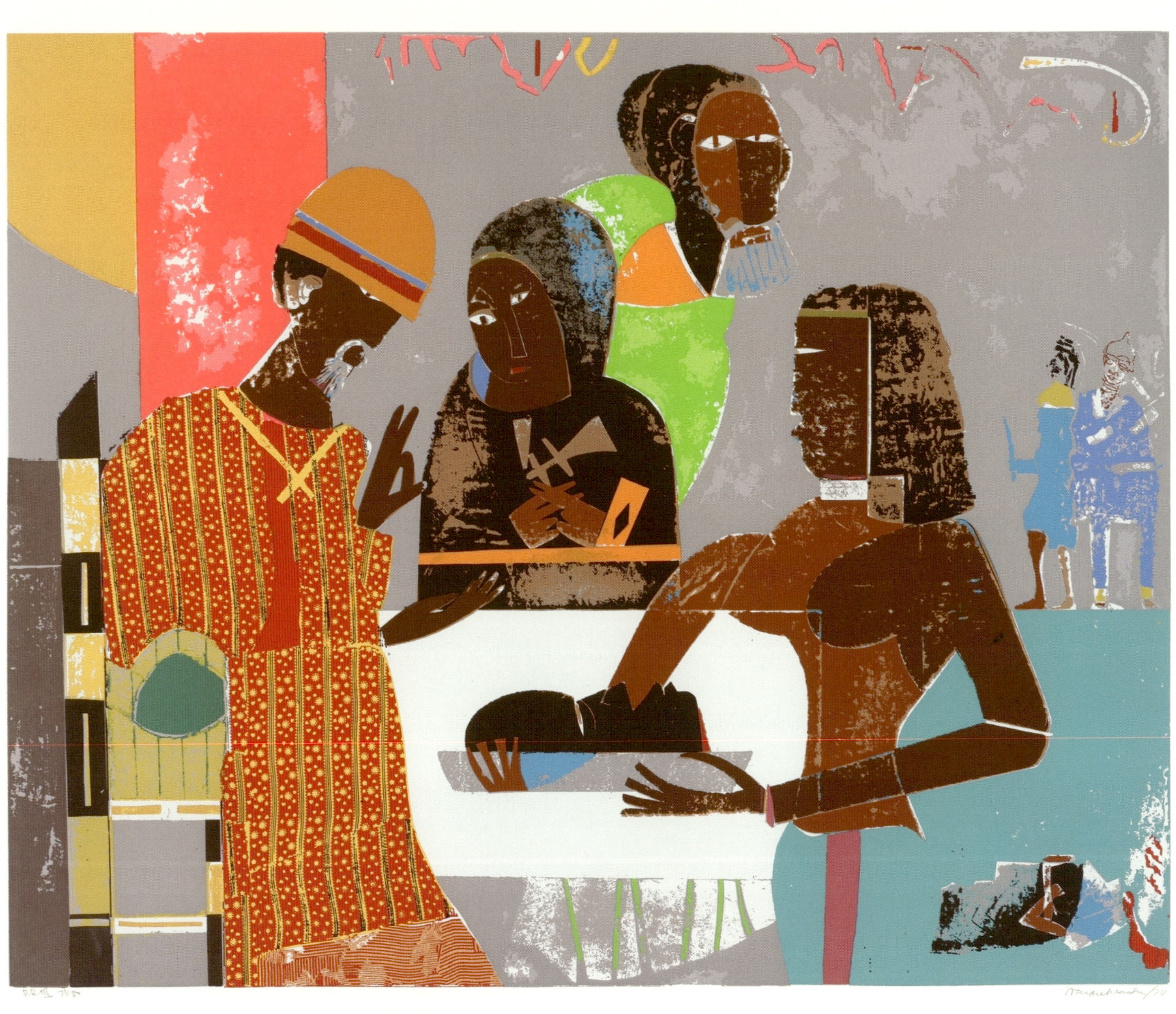

Romare Bearden (American, 1911–1988), *Prevalence of Ritual portfolio: Salome (John the Baptist)*, 1974, screenprint, 32⅛ x 40⅛ in.

Curators' Statement

Engaging a wide range of experiences and artistic practices, the nine artists featured in this exhibition challenge the controlling images of Black women that continue to pervade our culture and influence perceptions. Their artworks jar loose expectations and replace simplistic narratives with nuanced, sophisticated meditations on contemporary identity.

The essays in this publication similarly present a variety of perspectives on the artworks and the ideas they present. Contributions from a diverse group of accomplished scholars, activists, artists, and writers provide multiple viewpoints from which to consider the exhibition and the questions it presents. Together, the artists' works and the authors' voices reveal the complexity of identity, the necessity for self-determination, and the power of art to stimulate dialogue.

We would like to thank the artists featured in this exhibition for their artistically and socially groundbreaking works and the catalogue essayists for their thoughtful, personal, and artistic responses. Special thanks to the Jordan Schnitzer Family Foundation for providing the opportunity for Colorado College and the Alexandria Museum of Art to collaborate in the curation of this exhibition from the Foundation's world-class collection of prints.

Jessica Hunter-Larsen

DIRECTOR OF ACADEMIC ENGAGEMENT / CURATOR OF INTERDISCIPLINARY ARTS
COLORADO COLLEGE

Megan Valentine

CURATOR & REGISTRAR
ALEXANDRIA MUSEUM OF ART

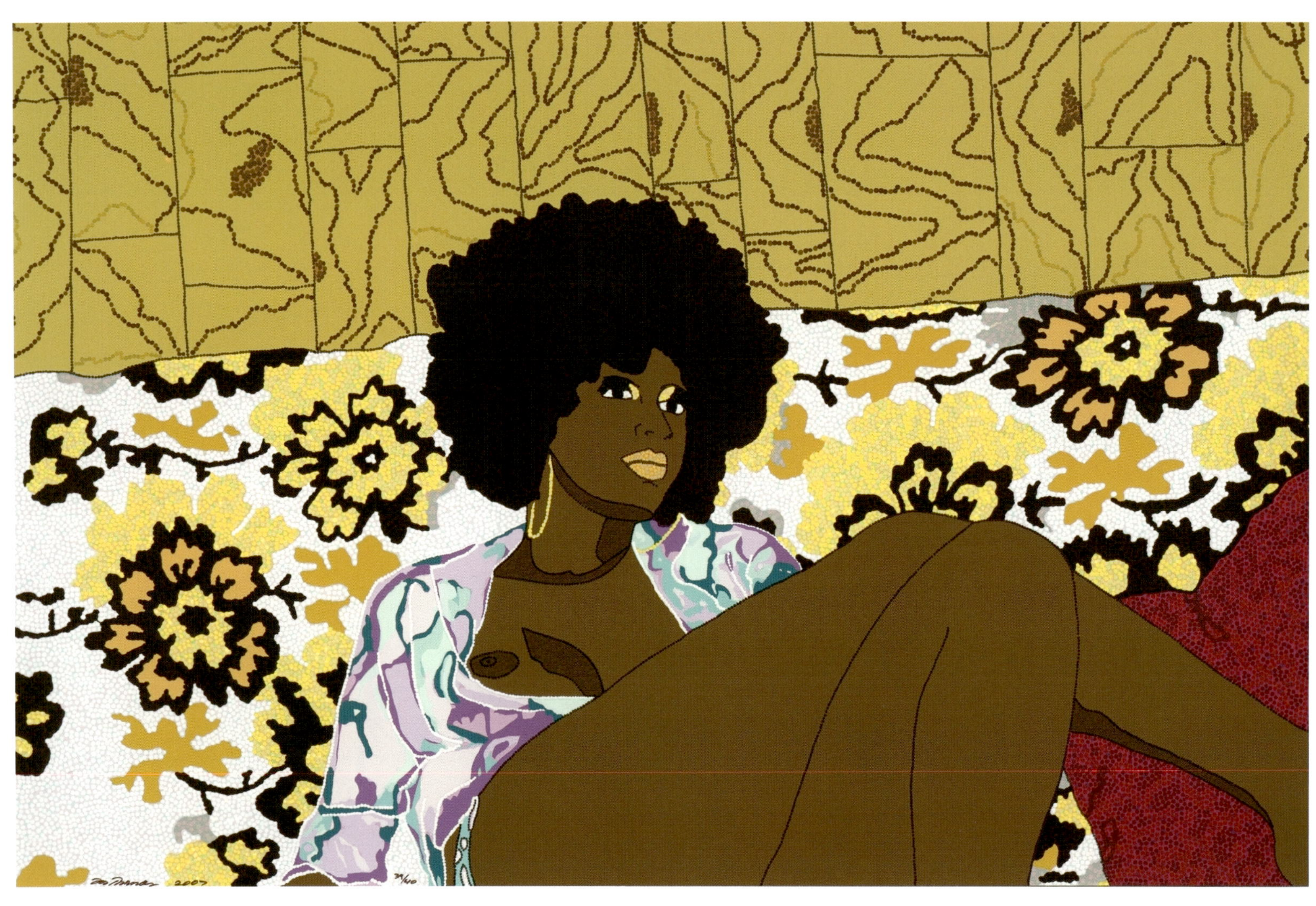

Mickalene Thomas (American, b. 1971), *Why Can't We Just Sit Down and Talk It Over*, 2006, screenprint, 19½ x 30 in. © Mickalene Thomas

Preface

Gaze at Me

We have long posed the question of whether art reflects the worldview of the time it was created or whether art influences that time. I think we can agree that both of these ideas are correct, depending on the artist and the work, as well as the reality of the environment that surrounds them.

Many artists have sought to reveal the untold truths of their time in their work. Some artists view their work as a form of activism when they are creating with social change as its impetus. Throughout history, we have witnessed art used as a form of propaganda to influence the beliefs of entire populations. Whether art was created to inspire understanding of those who are different, or to encourage fear and loathing of the *other*, art has proved an effective tool toward either goal.

Historically, we are also familiar with the long-established (and debated) idea of the male gaze, with the images of women in fine art, of any race, created predominantly by men and presented in a way that is pleasing to men. This sexual objectification of women permeates all art forms and media even today, in spite of feminist attempts at change. Although we live in a world where women have more opportunities and power, it is still very much "a man's world" and women are very aware. In the book *Ways of Seeing*, John Berger says "She has to survey everything she is and everything she does because how she appears to others, and ultimately how she appears to men, is of crucial importance for what is normally thought of as success in her life. Her own sense of being in herself is supplanted by a sense of being appreciated as herself by another…"[1]

Feminist artists and many contemporary artists have utilized the figure in their work to question and challenge these predisposed beliefs of beauty, race, gender, and sexuality, as well as censorship, morality, and ethics. The artists in this exhibition are presenting images of women of color, which superimposes the specific dynamic of race over the subject of

---

1   John Berger et al., *Ways of Seeing* (New York: Viking, 1972), 46.

woman. Not only have images of Black women been subject to the male gaze, but also to the predominantly white worldview and aesthetic of western art. This leaves us with images that have been created to fit into the stereotypes that are comfortable for whites while ignoring the realities of people of color. In the quote above from *Ways of Seeing*, we could easily substitute the word "whites" for the word "men" and see the truth in it. The artists in *Beyond Mammy, Jezebel & Sapphire: Reclaiming Images of Black Women* are predominantly Black women themselves and, as such, are asking us to open our eyes to the challenges they face both as Black women and artists.

In this exhibit, the only works produced prior to 2000 were created by male African American artists. Romare Bearden and Robert Colescott are both considered some of the most important artists of their time and have helped to break down barriers and bring attention to highly sensitive and political issues. While their provocative work often addresses issues of race identity as well as racial and sexual stereotypes, it is not until more recently that we see female African American artists tackling these topics in the mainstream. This speaks to the realities that face women artists regarding the lack of recognition in the art world, particularly inclusion in museums and galleries. The work of the Guerrilla Girls, founded in 1985, has brought attention to the discrepancy through the utilization of anonymously created billboards, posters, public action, books, and projects that confront the inequity using facts and humor. This group continues to reinvent feminism for the 21st century, focusing on social change and the lack of opportunities for women and artists of color. Along with other activists, they have opened the door for contemporary artists, who are women of color, to reclaim their own image.

Kara Walker, Wangechi Mutu, Mildred Howard, and Alison Saar all seize the subject matter of their work in a way that is unapologetic and candid. They often utilize familiar and stereotypical imagery in an affront to western standards of beauty imposed on them. Utilizing layers of storytelling, mythology, historical knowledge, and cultural signifiers, these artists force us to confront the social burden created by stereotypes like Mammy, Jezebel, and Sapphire. We might speculate that some of the artists in the exhibition may indeed be some of the anonymous Guerrilla Girls.

As a museum director, I believe that artists are fearless risk takers who can lead us to places we need to go in order to see the truth. For the viewer, I hope the images in this exhibition open up possibilities perhaps not considered before and encourage contemplation about the ways we view one another.

Catherine M. Pears

EXECUTIVE DIRECTOR

ALEXANDRIA MUSEUM OF ART

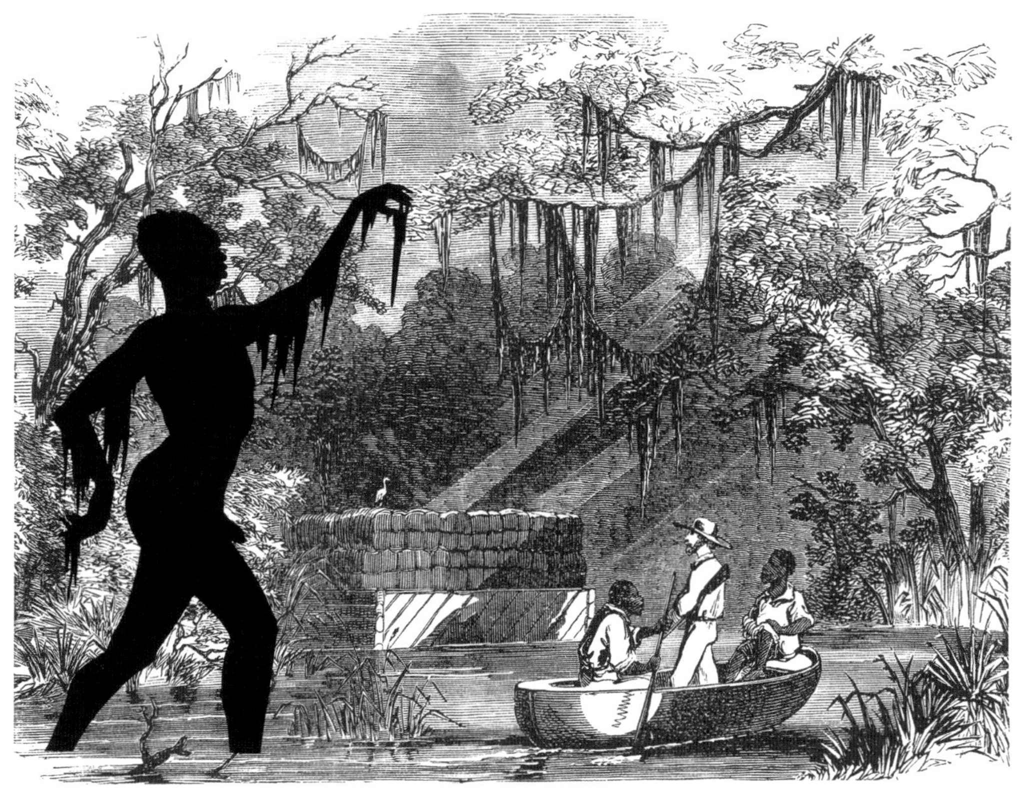

Kara Walker (American, b. 1969), *Harper's Pictorial History of the Civil War (Annotated): Cotton Hoards in Southern Swamp*, 2005, offset lithography and screenprint, 39 x 53 in. ©Kara Walker, courtesy of Sikkema Jenkins & Co., New York.

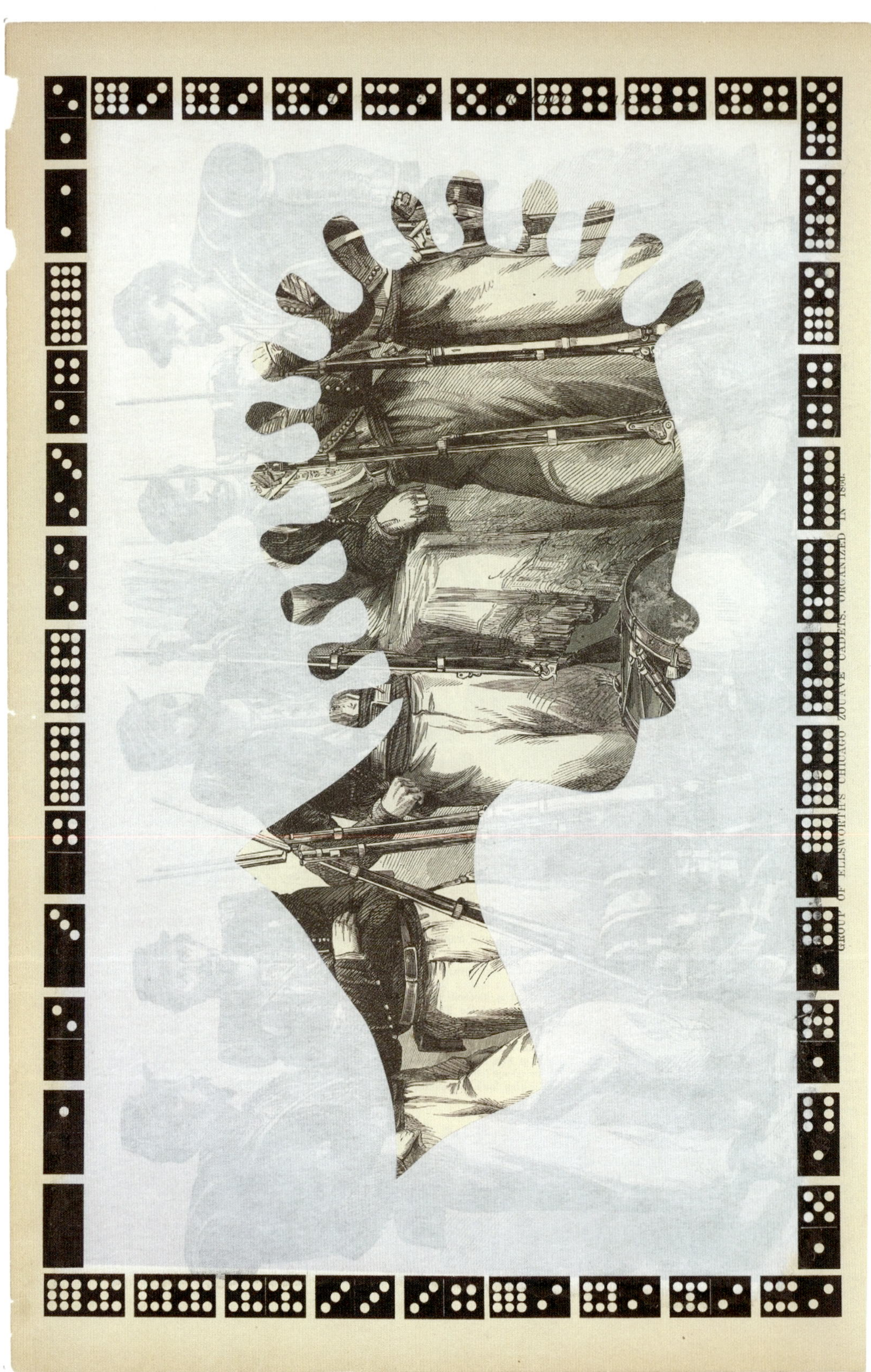

Mildred Howard (American, b. 1945), *I've Been a Witness to this Game III*, 2016, color monoprint/digital on found paper with collage, 20⅝ x 15⅛ in.

Who Will Sing a Black Girl's Song?

A Case for Black Feminist and Womanist Exhibit Engagement

Heidi R. Lewis

A good job has been done in this country, as far as convincing [Black women] of their inferiority is concerned. The general white community has told us in a million different ways and in no uncertain terms that "God" and "nature" made a mistake when it came to fashioning us and ours.

— ABBEY LINCOLN, "Who Will Revere the Black Woman?" (1966)

No other creative field is as closed to those who are not white and male as is the visual arts. After I decided to be an artist, the first thing that I had to believe was that I, a black woman, could penetrate the art scene, and that, further, I could do so without sacrificing one iota of my blackness or my femaleness or my humanity.

— FAITH RINGGOLD, *Ms.* Magazine Interview (1973)

BANTU KNOTS, sew-in weaves, Egyptian cuts, baldies, perms, Afros, bald fades, plaits.

Unfortunately, only an exhibit that *centers* Black women as artists and subjects of artistic expression would typically invite audiences to see and appreciate these hairstyles and the Black women who wear them in this kind of artistic space. And while hair is but one way in which Black womanhood is defined and expressed, and sometimes overdetermined both within and outside Black communities, it is through this particular aesthetic vehicle that I invite audiences — albeit briefly — to understand and appreciate *Beyond Mammy, Jezebel & Sapphire: Reclaiming*

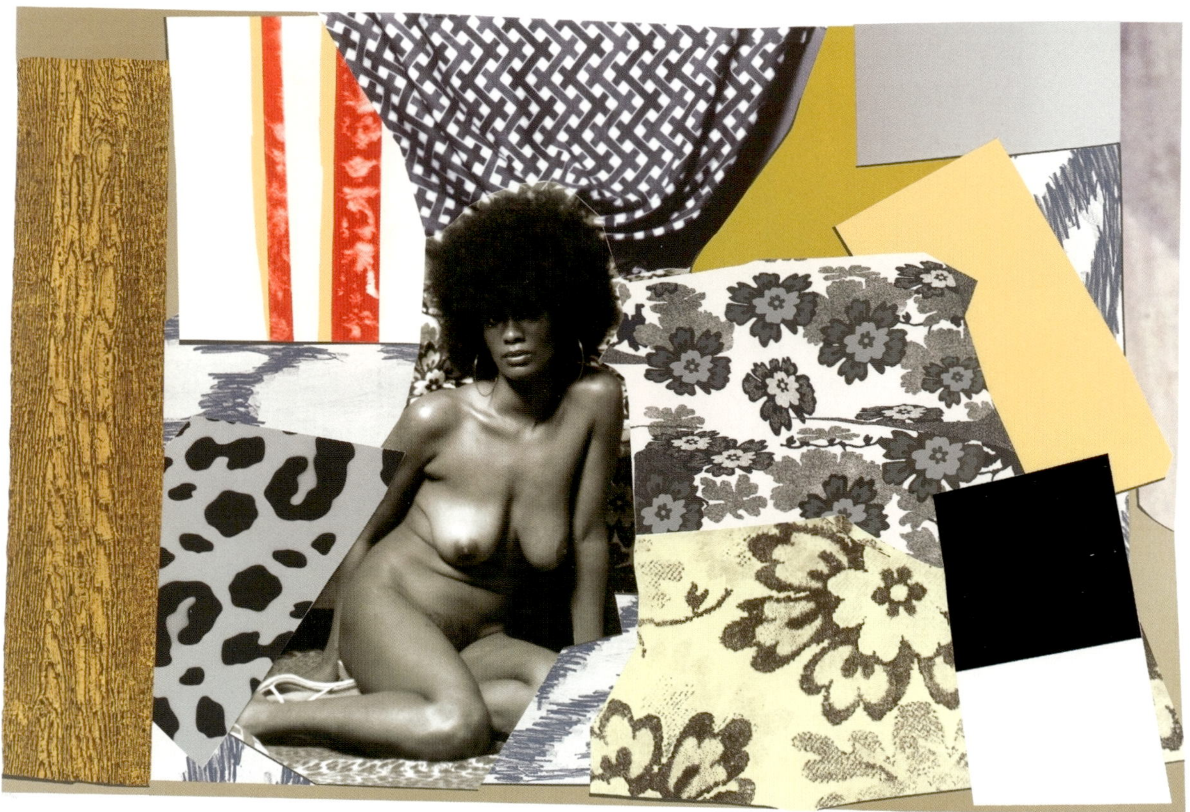

Mickalene Thomas (American, b. 1971), *Left Behind Again 2*, 2014, relief, intaglio, lithography, digital, collage, enamel paint, 44 x 65¼ in.

Images of Black Women, as well as the Black women it honors, by employing a deliberately Black feminist and womanist lens. I make this case, because for nearly 250 years (long before the terms feminism and womanism were created), these frameworks have implored us to seriously consider and address the ways in which racism, sexism, heterosexism, and other forms of visible and invisible, explicit and dysconscious oppression interconnect and shape our experiences. Along these lines, Patricia Hill Collins advances a Black feminist epistemology that implores us to "distinguish what has been said about subordinated groups in the dominant discourse, and what such groups might say about themselves if given the opportunity." Further, Layli Maparyan defines womanism as "a space of redemption for the genius of everyday folk, beginning but not ending with women, especially women of color."

I became acutely aware of the need for such redemption not long before I turned five years old and started kindergarten at North Lincoln Elementary School in Alliance, Ohio. For the occasion, especially momentous since I was permitted to quit preschool after one day and never went to daycare, my mother dressed me in a supremely frilly, but very pretty, yellow or pink first-day-of-school dress with complementary white, patent leather shoes and a white bow clipped to my hair. Being that it was 1986, it would likely surprise no Black person living in the U.S. that my hair was styled in a Jheri Curl, created by entrepreneur Comer Cottrell and named for hairstylist, chemist, and entrepreneur William "Jheri" Redding. The Jheri Curl — popularized throughout the 1970s and '80s by Black entertainers, such as Rick James, Debbie Allen, Michael Jackson, Evelyn "Champagne" King, Eazy-E, and Ola Ray — was hailed as a "wash and wear" style much easier to manage than natural Black hair or other chemical straightening treatments like the "relaxer." The Jheri Curl gave its wearers glossy curls — tight or loose, depending on the size of the chosen curling rods — that would shine after the user applied the appropriate amount of curl "activator." On my first day of school, my curls were shining brightly, so my hair was super greasy, which posed a bit of a problem for the Big Bird poster I leaned on as I waited to enter my classroom. As a result, two white boys standing behind me found this an appropriate occasion for bullying. They snickered. They laughed. They whispered. They pointed. And I was mortified. Up until that point, my family and community taught me to know myself as a curious, smart, beautiful, funny, and loved little Black girl. At that moment, those boys taught me that I was one thing and one thing only: ugly.

Thirty years later, we have strong evidence that Black women and girls are still aesthetically subjugated, especially concerning their various hairstyles. For example, in September 2013, Tiana Parker, a then seven year old girl in Tulsa, Oklahoma, was sent home from her Black-led charter school because, according to school policy, her dreadlocks were "unacceptable." This past May, Marian Reed's nine year old daughter was called into the office at Tarver Elementary School in Temple, Texas, because the Assistant Principal claimed her natural hair looked like a "faux hawk," which violates school dress code. This problem is not unique to Black girls in the U.S., however, as this past February, a group of Black girls were suspended from the C.R. Walker Senior High School in Nassau, Bahamas, because their natural hair was deemed "untidy, ungroomed, and unkempt." Similarly, in 2015, the mother of a thirteen-year-old student in Toronto, Canada was told by Principal Tracey Barnes, a Black woman, that her daughter's hair was "too poofy" and "unprofessional." Sadly, this subjugation likely will not cease when these girls become women. We know this because of Jessica Sims, Far-ryn Johnson, Rhonda Lee, Ashley Davis, and the scores of other Black women who were shamed — as I was at four years old — and materially affected by the assumption that their bodies, especially their hair, "threaten the social, political, and economic fabric of American life," as Paulette M. Caldwell points out.

Beyond Mammy, Jezebel & Sapphire, then, should inspire audiences to think critically about these and the many other dangerous assumptions about Black women in ways that are far more complex than discourses outside of Black feminism and womanism typically allow. A large part of that work entails listening intently to the ways Black women, including the artists featured here, think about and discuss ourselves on our own terms, which is critical, because as the late Black, lesbian, mother, warrior, poet Audre Lorde reminds us on behalf of all Black women, "If I did not define myself for myself, I would be crunched into other people's fantasies for me and eaten alive." It is important, then, for us to spend some time here — and hopefully more time as we continue to engage the exhibit — hearing some of

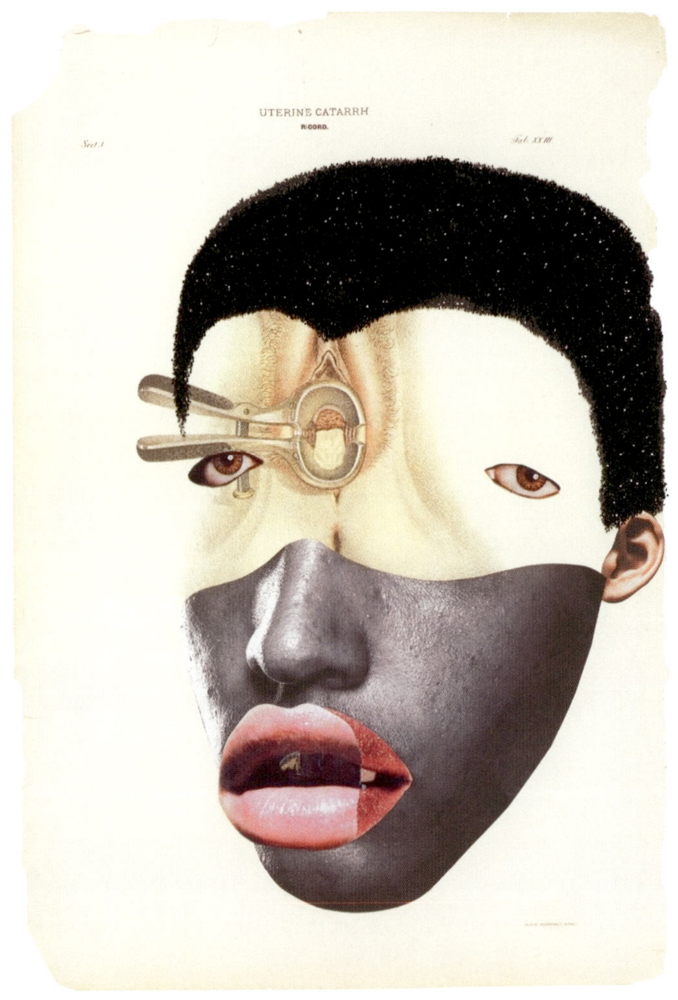

Wangechi Mutu (Kenyan, b. 1972), *Histology of the Different Classes of Uterine Tumors: Uterine Catarrh* (detail), 2006, glitter, ink, collage on found medical illustration paper, 23 x 17 in.

these Black women artists speak for themselves. Along these lines, Kara Walker tells us, "Challenging and highlighting abusive power dynamics in our culture is my goal; replicating them is not." Wangechi Mutu notes, "A lot of my work reflects the incredible influence that America has had on contemporary African culture. Some of it's insidious, some of it's innocuous, some of it's invisible." And Alison Saar claims, "The balance of the work has been political, but coming from very much my own personal experience and personal point of view as a woman, as a mother, as an African American." Hence, to fully appreciate Walker, one *must* be intensely aware of the "abusive power dynamics in our culture" that she is working to resist. In order to appreciate Mutu, one *must* be aware of and pay *careful* attention to the "incredible influence" America has had on African culture. To better understand the significance of Saar, one *must* acknowledge the historical and contemporary social, cultural, and political contexts that inform her experiences as woman, mother, and African American. And of course, these abusive power dynamics, influences, and contexts undoubtedly include the Mammy, Jezebel, Sapphire, Strong Black Woman, Welfare Queen, Hoochie, Bitch, Ho, Side Chick, Chickenhead, and other disparaging caricatures of Black women no matter how complimentary they may seem or how the names vary depending on geographical location, time period, and other determinants.

The two little boys at my elementary school were reared in a culture in which these caricatures and their implications continue to have a significant impact on Black women—within and outside Black communities—and in which understanding Black womanhood and caring deeply about Black women continues to have little to no importance. The same is true for the aforementioned school officials and employers who decided that the myriad ways Black women and girls express themselves aesthetically through their hair was not worth knowing and understanding, let alone appreciating. We know this to be true if we listen carefully to and *believe* the Black women who are pleading with us to #SayHerName and who scream #BlackWomenMatter and #BlackGirlsRock. It is my hope, then, that audiences engaging this exhibit will take a moment to take part in this listening, this *believing* by singing a Black girl's song, by sharing in a counternarrative that does know, understand, and appreciate the complexity of Black women's pain, Black women's joy, Black women's trauma, Black women's healing, Black women's tears, Black women's laughs, Black women's souls, Black women's spirits, Black women's minds, Black women's emotions, Black women's intellect, Black women's skin, Black women's shape, Black women's hair. As Toni Morrison writes in *The Bluest Eye* (1970), "Guileless and without vanity, we were still in love with ourselves then. We felt comfortable in our own skins, enjoyed the news that our senses released to us, admired our dirt, cultivated our scars, and could not comprehend this unworthiness." The artists featured in *Beyond Mammy, Jezebel & Sapphire* are attempting to create a space in which Black women can remain forever in love with ourselves and comfortable in our own skins, inspired by our dirt and scars and uninhibited by tales of our unworthiness.

––––––––––

Heidi R. Lewis, PhD is an Assistant Professor of Feminist & Gender Studies at Colorado College and an Associate Editor for *The Feminist Wire* whose work primarily focuses on Feminist Theory, Critical Race Theory, and Critical Media Studies. She has been published in *The Cultural Impact of Kanye West* and the *Journal of Popular Culture*, and has given talks at Kim Bevill's Gender and the Brain Conference, the Educating Children of Color Summit, the Motherhood Initiative for Research and Community Involvement, the Gender and Media Spring Convocation at Ohio University, and the Conference for Pre-Tenure Women at Purdue University, where she earned a PhD in American Studies with a minor in Women's, Gender, & Sexuality Studies. She has also been a contributor to Mark Anthony Neal's *NewBlackMan*, *NPR*'s "Here and Now," KOAA news, KRCC radio, *Bitch Media*, *Racialicious*, and *Act Out*.

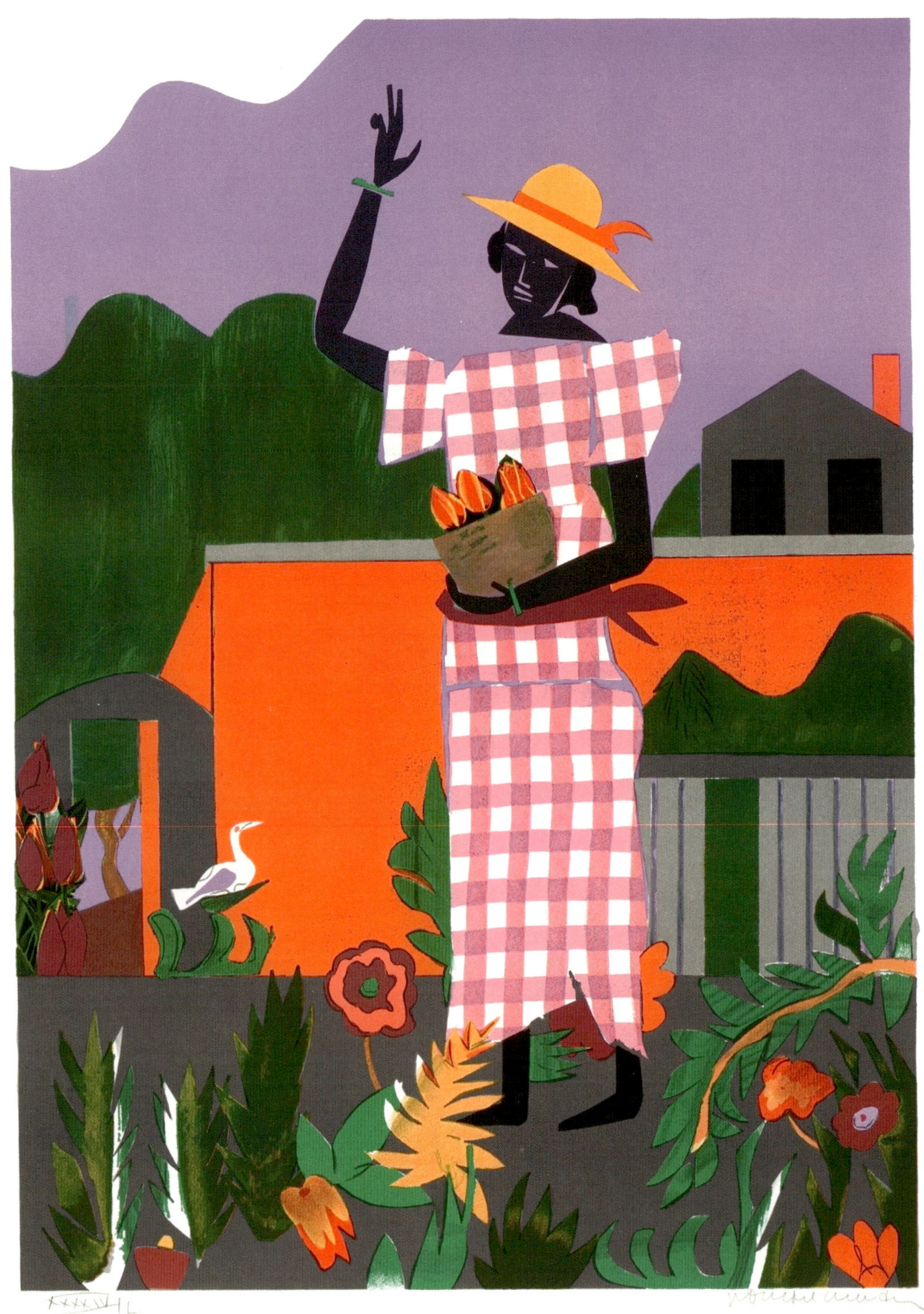

Romare Bearden (American, 1911–1988), *American Portfolio: Girl in the Garden*, 1980, silkscreen, 28½ x 21 in.

Beyond Mammy, Jezebel & Sapphire: Reclaiming Images of Black Women

Roland W. Mitchell

We do not really see through our eyes or hear through our ears, but through our beliefs. To put our beliefs on hold is to cease to exist as ourselves for a moment — and that is not easy … but it is the only way to learn what it might feel like to be someone else and the only way to start the dialogue

—LISA DELPIT, 2012

The quote above is by beloved theorist, Southern University professor, and Native Louisianan Lisa Delpit. Her insightful recognition of the power of belief to shape our perceptions and relationship to others is a fruitful place for engaging the visually stunning and emotionally stirring exhibit *Beyond Mammy, Jezebel & Sapphire: Reclaiming Images of Black Women*. Delpit's interrogation of our sensual engagement of beliefs about the *Other* provides a critical starting point for dialogue across the varying manner in which Black women's ways of being and knowing have been historically cast as simultaneously highly visible yet peculiarly absent in mainstream U.S. discourse. Reclaiming the rich, imaginative, and socially engaged energies that gave rise to contemporary representations of Black women undergirds the challenge put forth by the exhibit to move beyond shallow caricatures of Black women as reflected in the mammy, jezebel, and sapphire. Therefore, as you consider the pieces in the exhibit we challenge you to take Delpit up on her charge "to put our beliefs on hold," and engage upon a culturally informed reclaiming of images of Black women.

The Mammy, Jezebel, and Sapphire.

Donald Bogle's classic *Toms, Coons, Mulattoes, Mammies & Bucks: An Interpretive History of Blacks in Films* (1973), introduces five pervasive categories (as referenced in the title of the text) as the primary archetypes for contemporary popular culture images of Black people in America. Despite the fact that these images predate the Constitution and were actually solidified in the Civil War era, their propagation in the early 20th century went hand in hand—and many would argue significantly advanced—the development and popularization of motion picture technology. Consequently during this era, the ability to mass produce simplistic and most often derogatory images of Black people for consumption by an ill-informed white public went hand in hand with intersecting oppressions of racism and sexism. Infamous illustrations of these machinations can be found in wildly popular early motion pictures like D. W. Griffith's 1915 *Birth of a Nation*.

During this emergent era of U.S. popular culture, the mammy most prominently displayed by Hattie McDaniel's Academy Award winning role in Margaret Mitchell's 1939 *Gone with the Wind*, served as the pattern for the jezebel and sapphire images of Black women. Mammy, or "Aunt Jemima," was the fiercely independent, portly, desexualized domestic who was every white person's favorite grandmother. This depiction of Black women often presented mammy as more nurturing and loyal to the white family who she faithfully served than she was to her own kin (Yarbrough and Bennett, 2005). Jezebel on the other hand, was equally independent but she was framed as seductive, cunning, and as the biblical reference implies, an exotic temptress whose mesmerizing sensuality is the antithesis of the innocence and piety attributed to the "true womanhood" (Perkins, 1983) of affluent white women. Sapphire took mammy's and jezebel's independent spirit to another level, often portrayed hands on hips, head thrown back; an emasculating and cantankerous woman who let all—man, woman, and child—know she's in charge.

Despite the fact that Black women had no input on these images, and for the most part it was not until the 1920s that Black people even portrayed these roles in film, they were broadcast as true-to-life representations. However, social theorists suggest that as opposed to bearing any *true* resemblance to Black women, these architypes more closely reflected white anxieties about the evolving societal implications of strident attempts by Black people and women in particular to fully participate in post-Civil War America (Anderson, 1998; Davis, 2005). From this vantage, consider mammy as "happy to be in service," to alleviate white guilt about the inhumane treatment of Black people during slavery. Post emancipation however, the jezebel image arises out of countervailing racialized and gendered tensions placing Black and white women in a comparative context of white patriarchal desire. Women in general were challenging men for political, social, and economic parity and as the *weaker sex* and *inferior race* the jezebel image of Black women portrayed them as using their alluring and insatiable sexuality to overshadow white female virtue and manipulate male desire. And finally sapphire moved past mammy as the servant and jezebel as the siren to simply be the no-holds-barred evil harbinger of what would happen if the *natural* patriarchal and racial societal order was destabilized by granting women and Black people equality.

Reclaiming Images of Black Women

Engaging in contemporary struggles to reclaim images of Black women opens a space from which to critically consider societal beliefs about Black women. Following Delpit's charge in the opening quote, as you are drawn in by the pieces in the exhibit we challenge you to suspended deeply engrained ideas about Black women. Instead, enter this art not simply through your eyes and related physical senses but more profoundly through an interrogation of your beliefs. Further, view the exhibit as Delpit would assert, with an explicit focus on being a part of a dialogue. Historically this dialogue has been incomplete because images of Black women have been disproportionately shaped and propagated by others. Despite the pervasiveness of these farcical representations, Black women have historically and continuingly today self-authored their images. So a central part of the work of Black women reclaiming their representation means combatting patriarchal and racially informed fantasies of the mammy, jezebel, and sapphire through inclusions of the very real images and stories of Black women like Anna Julia Cooper, distinguished scholar and educator; Josephine St. Pierre, newspaper editor and philanthropist; and Augusta Savage and Lois Mailou Jones, both artists of Harlem Renaissance renown. And as the dialogue by Black women about Black women progresses to the 21st century, the voices of luminaries of social justice like Bernice Johnson Reagon and Marian Wright Edelman as well as contemporary popular culture icons like model-turned-DJ and creator of the nonprofit organization Black Girls Rock, Beverly Bond, must be celebrated as well. The fact that in 2020, in honor of the women's suffrage movement, abolitionist Sojourner Truth will be the first woman and person of color on U.S. currency suggests that this exhibit exists at the forefront of a national movement to not only reclaim but actually re-vision the image and participation of Black women in America. No doubt mammy and her offshoots are an important part of this reclaiming because they represent America's nascent imaginings about Black women. However, now the diversity of images in the exhibit paired with contemporary discourses about Black women establishes a rich and innovative venue for Black women to speak back in a manner that does justice to the power, brilliance, and countless contributions of the individuals who actually inspired the images.

REFERENCES

Anderson, J. (1988). *The Education of Blacks In The South 1860–1935*. Chapel Hill, NC: University of North Carolina Press.

Bogle, D. (1977). *Toms, Coons, Mulattoes, Mammies & Bucks: An Interpretive History of Blacks in Films*. New York: Continuum Press.

Davis, A. (2005). *Abolition Democracy Beyond Empire, Prison, and Torture*. New York: Seven Stories Press.

Goldstein, D. (2012). An interview with Lisa Delpit on educating 'other people's children.' *The Nation*. Retrieved September 10, 2016, from https://www.thenation.com/article/interview-lisa-delpit-educating-other-peoples-children/

Perkins, L. (1983). The impact of the "Cult of True Womanhood" on the education of Black Women. *Journal of Social Issues* 39(3): 154–159.

Yarbrough, M. & C, Bennett. (Spring 2000). Cassandra and the "Sistahs": The peculiar treatment of African American women in the myth of women as liars. *Journal of Gender, Race and Justice* 626–657, 634–655.

Roland W. Mitchell is the Jo Ellen Levy Endowed Professor and Associate Dean of Research and Academic Services in the College of Human Sciences and Education at Louisiana State University. He is Co-editor of the Lexington Press at Rowman & Littlefield for the book series Race and Education in the 21st Century, and Higher Education section editor of the *Journal of Curriculum Theorizing*.

Romare Bearden (American, 1911–1988), *The Train*, 1974, etching and aquatint, 22¼ x 30 in.

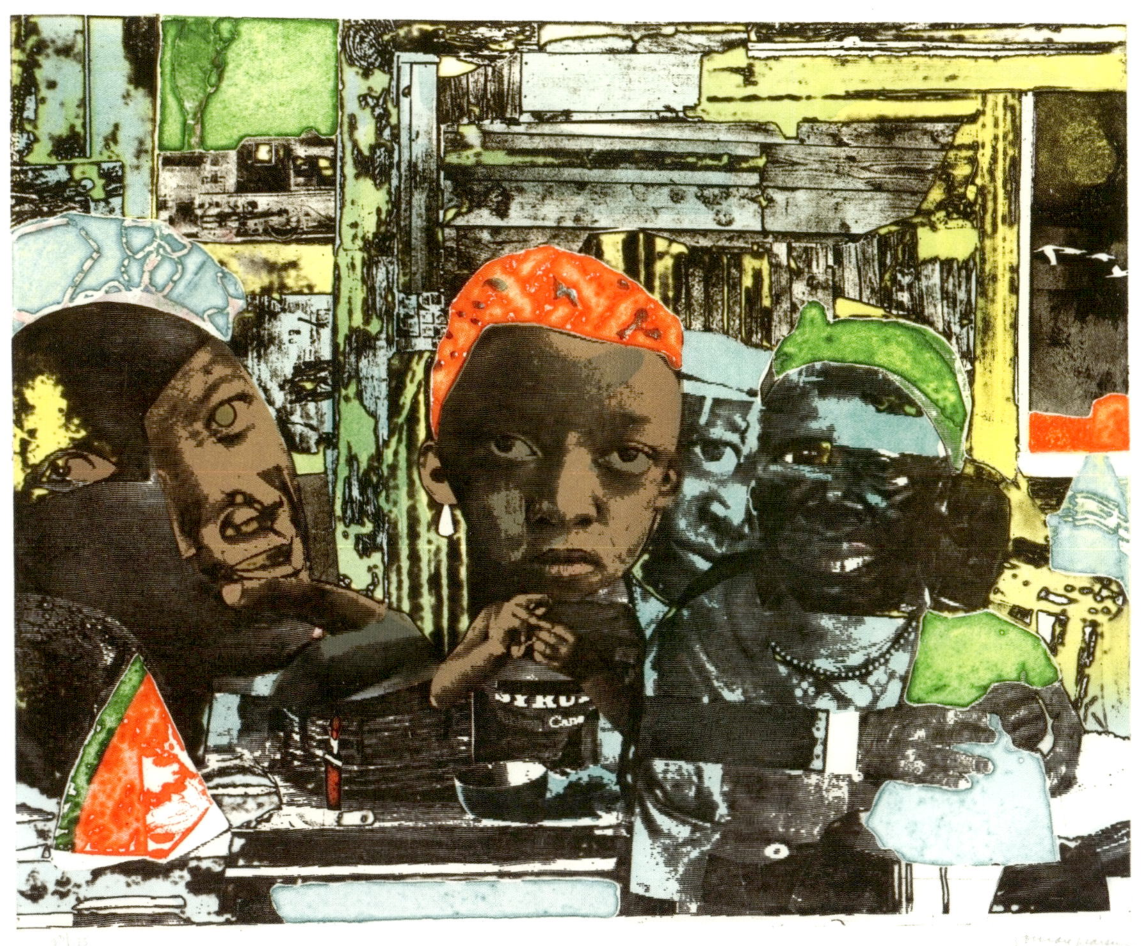

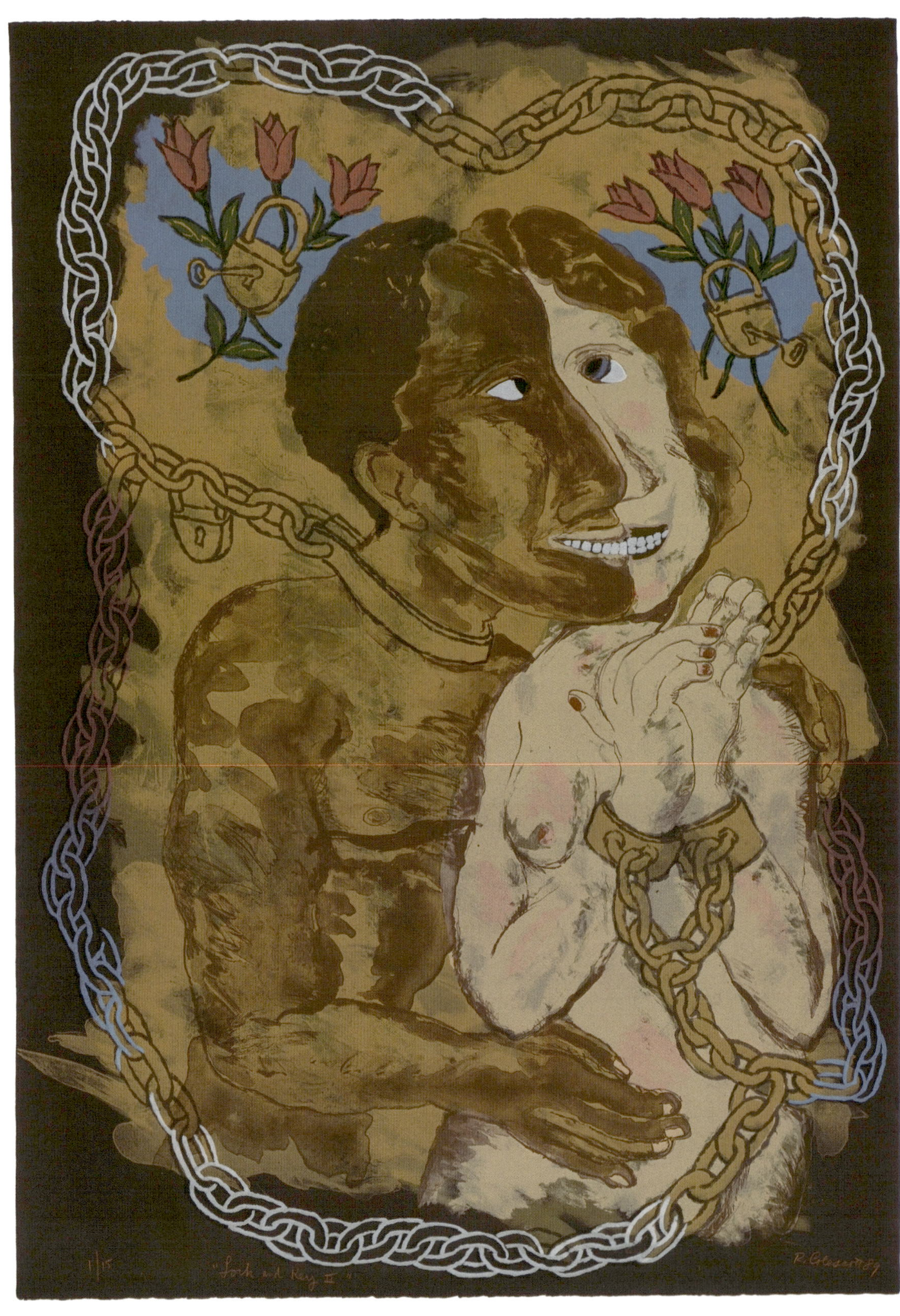

Robert Colescott (American, 1925–2009), *Lock and Key II*, 1989, lithograph, 42 x 30 in.

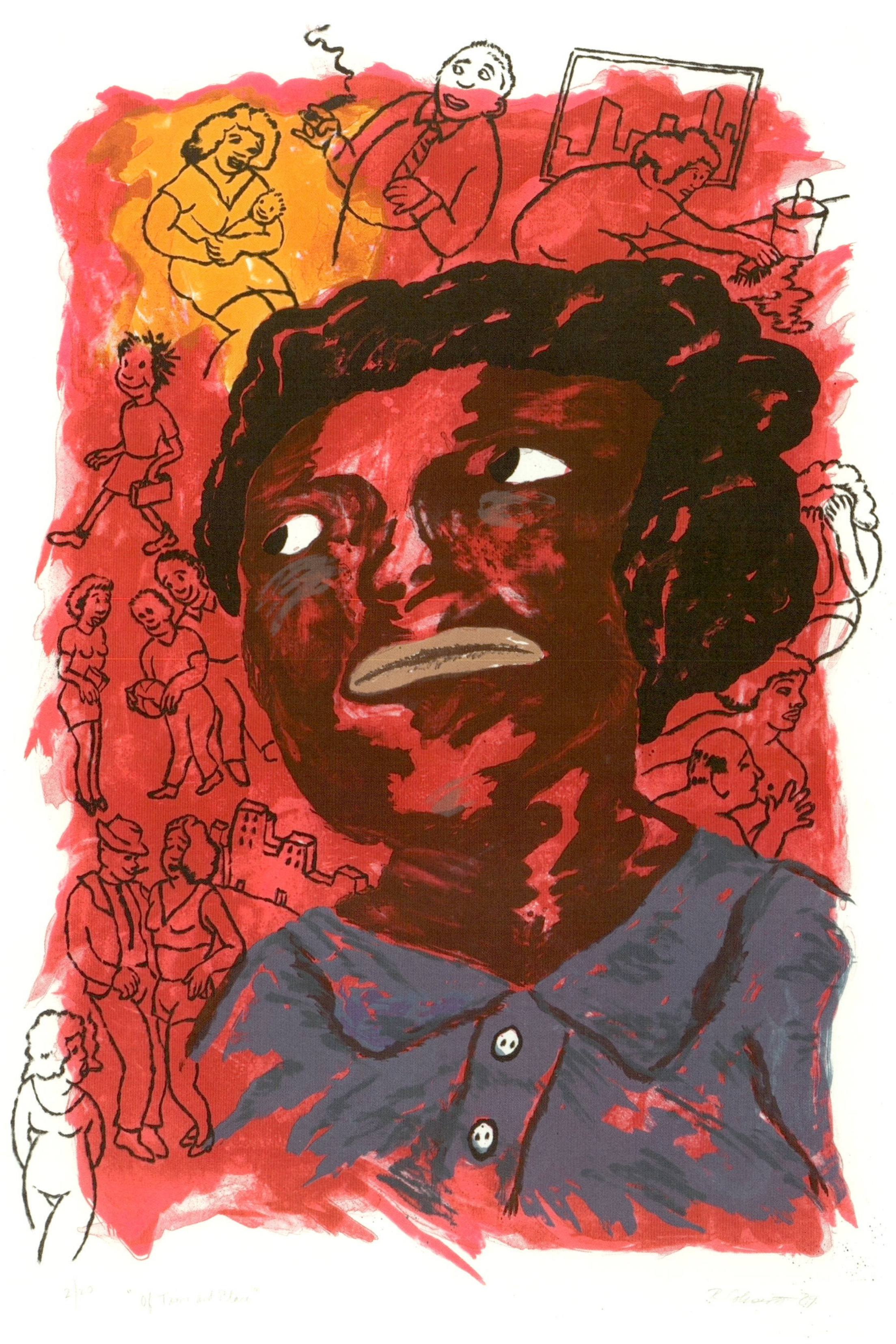

Robert Colescott (American, 1925–2009), *Of Time and Place*, 1989, lithograph, 42⅜ x 30¼ in.

Ellen Gallagher (American, b. 1965), *Ssblak! Ssblak!! Ssblakallblak! Wonder #9: Image #V,* 2000, screenprint, hardground etching, lithograph, 29⅞ x 28⅛ in.

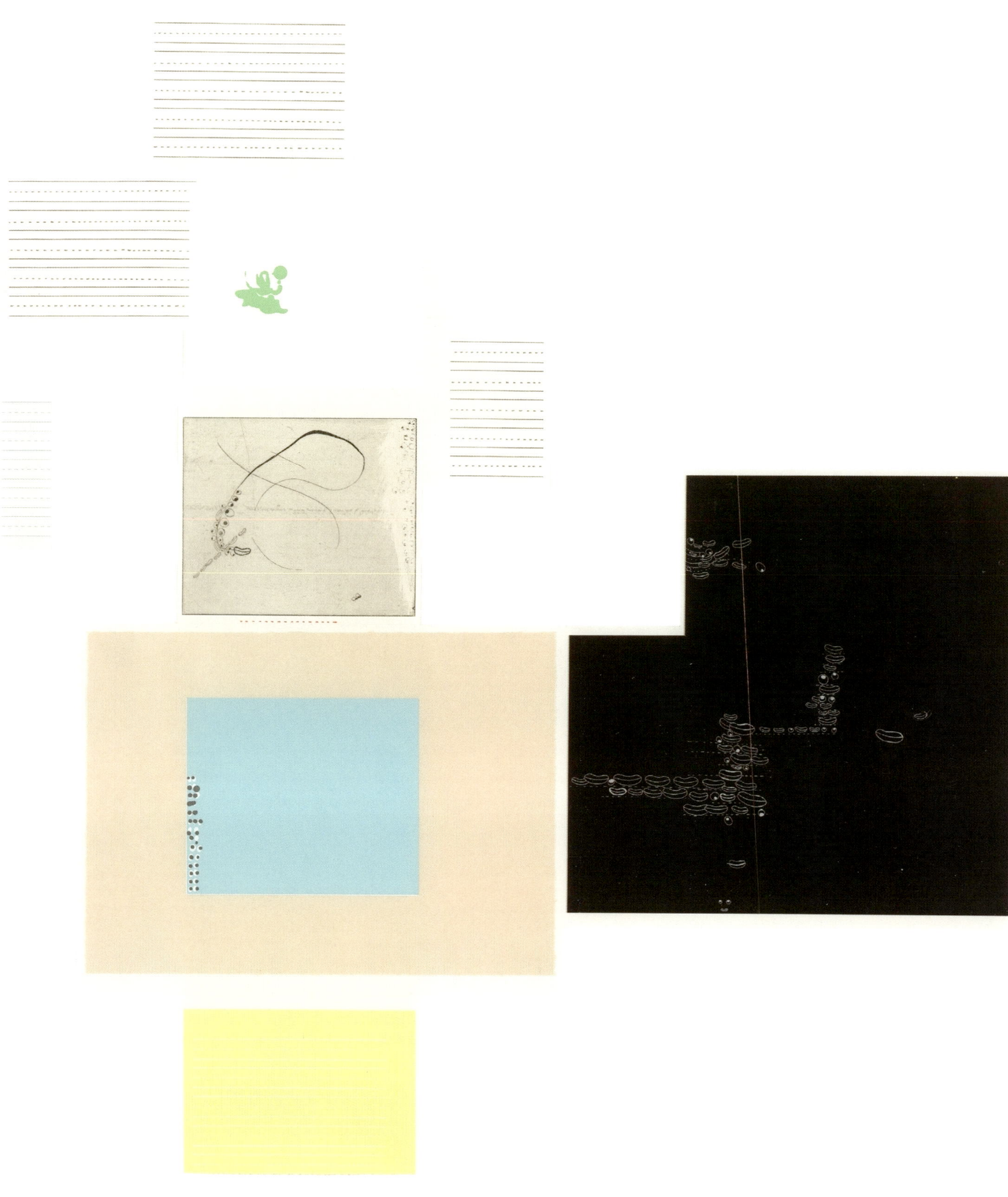

Ellen Gallagher (American, b. 1965), *Untitled (3)*, 2000, Ink on paper, 37 ¾ x 27 x 1 ¼ inches (95.9 x 68.6 x 3.2 cm) © Ellen Gallagher. Courtesy Gagosian.

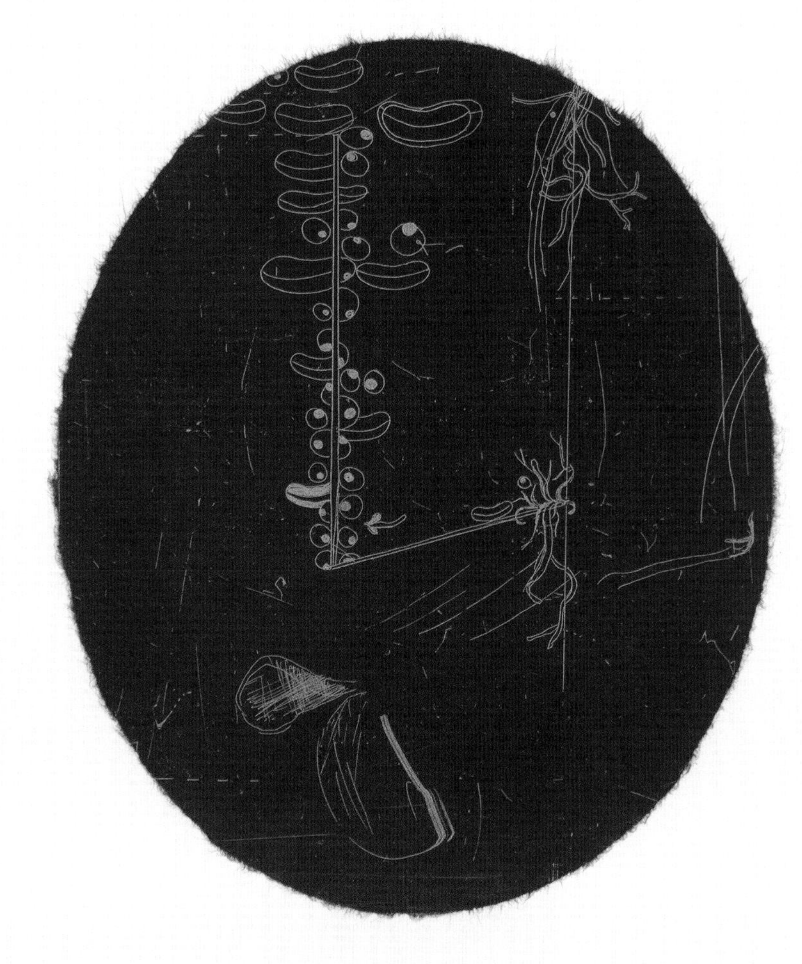

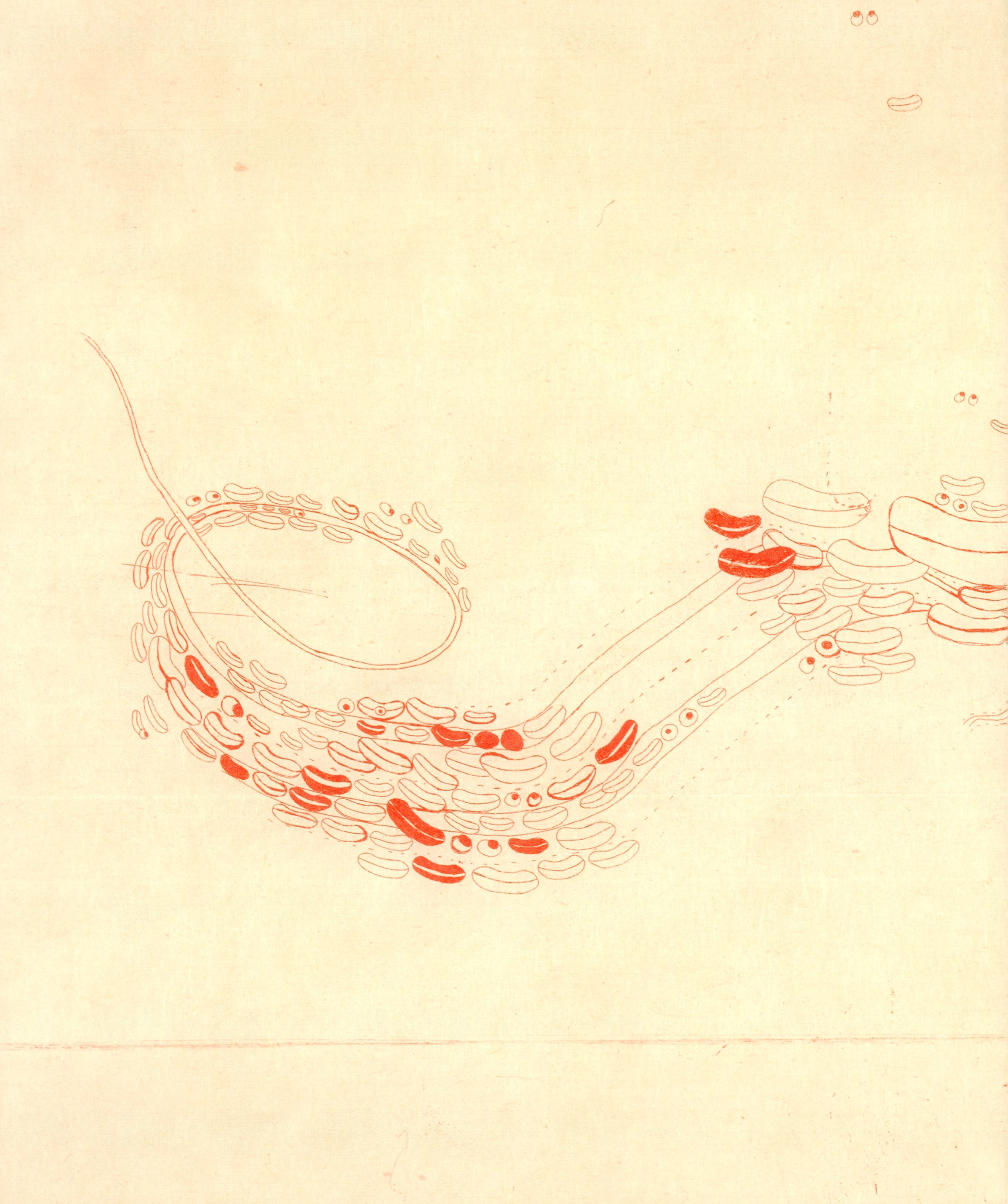

Ellen Gallagher (American, b. 1965), *Untitled* (8)(detail), 2000, Ink on paper, 37 ¾ x 27 x 1 ¼ inches (95.9 x 68.6 x 3.2 cm) © Ellen Gallagher. Courtesy Gagosian.

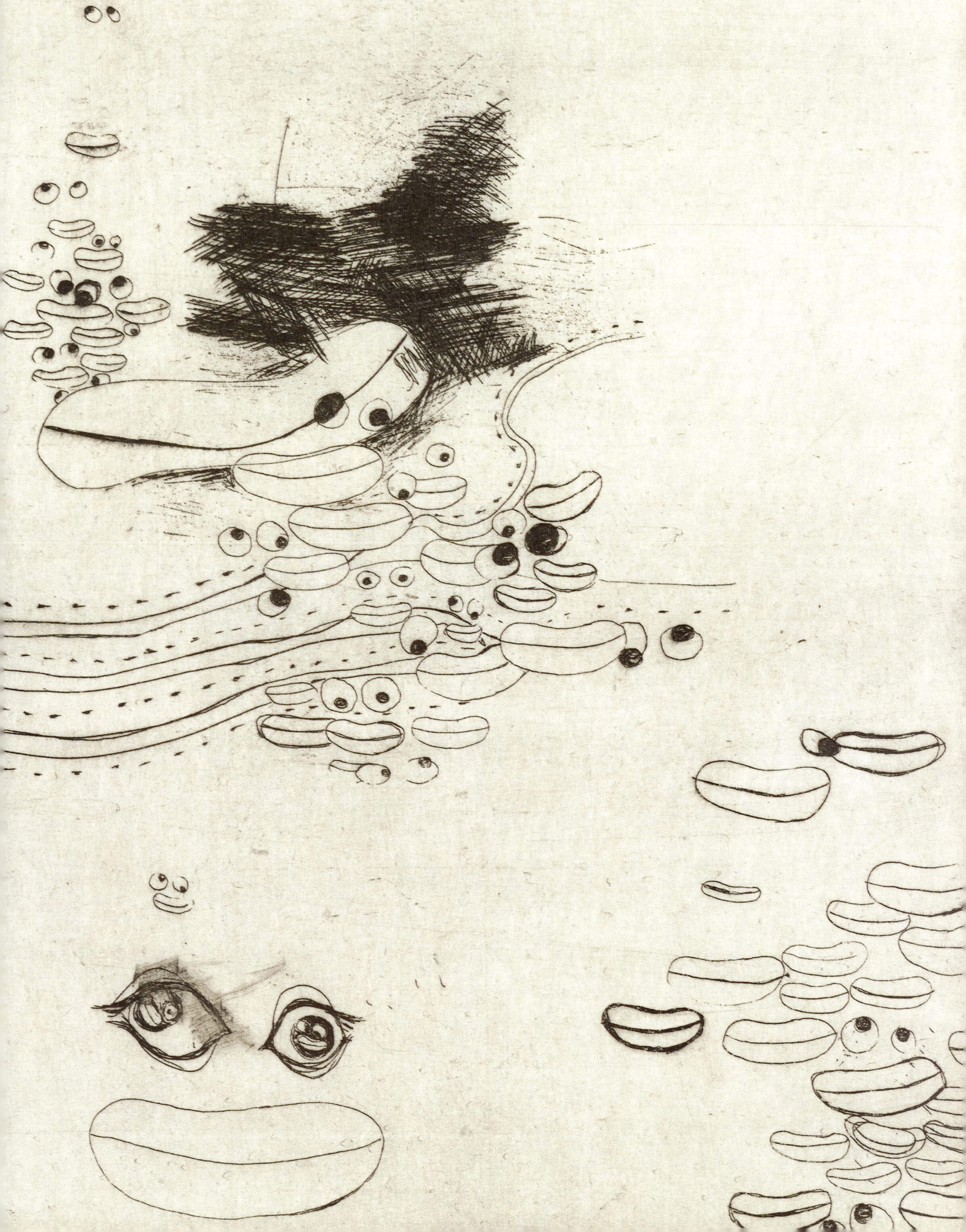

Mildred Howard (American, b. 1945), *I've Been a Witness to this Game IX*, 2016, color monoprint/digital on found paper with collage, 20⅝ x 15⅛ in.

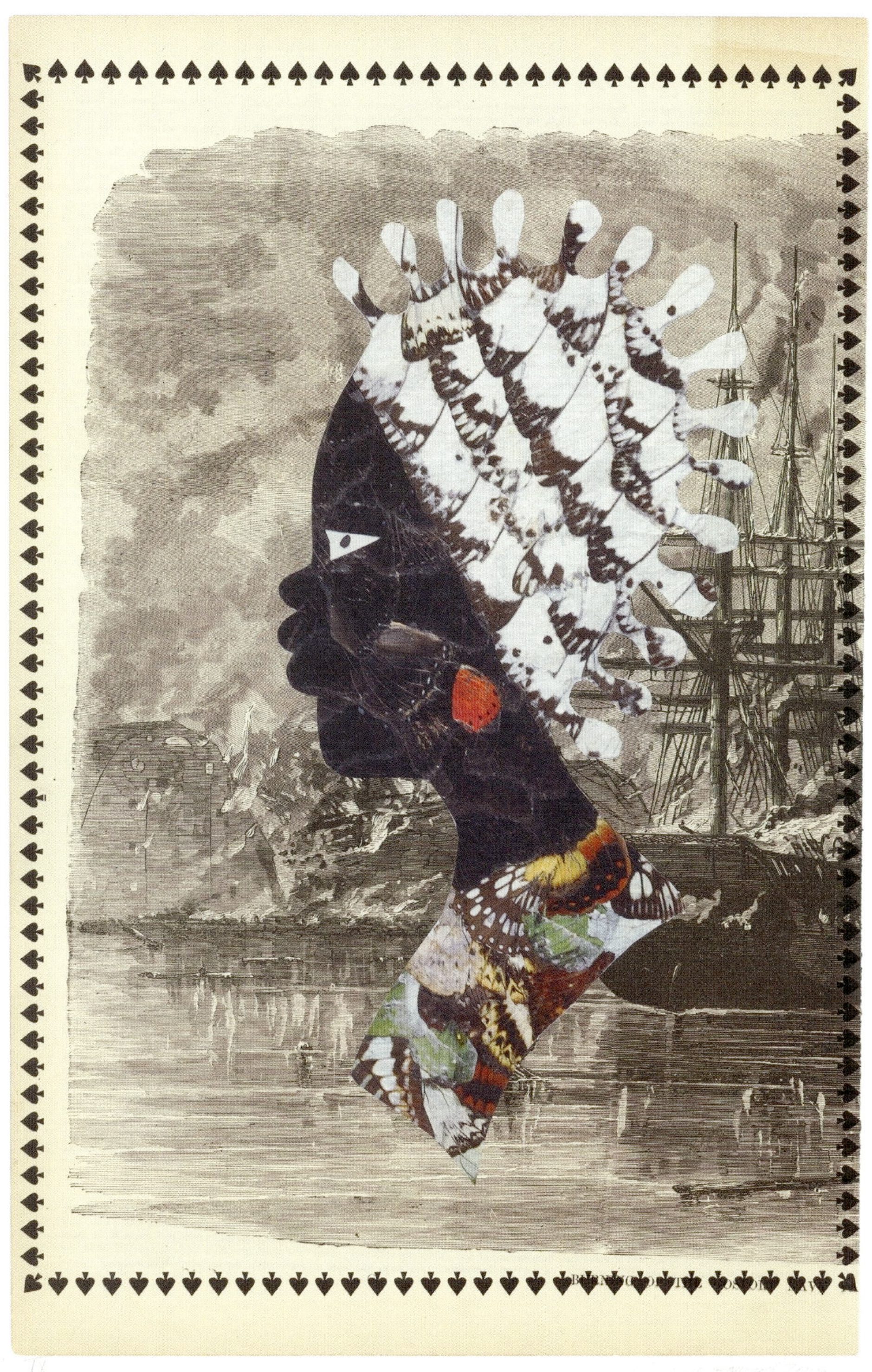

Mildred Howard (American, b. 1945), *I've Been a Witness to this Game XV*, 2016, color monoprint/digital with collage and gold leaf, 20⅝ x 15⅛ in.

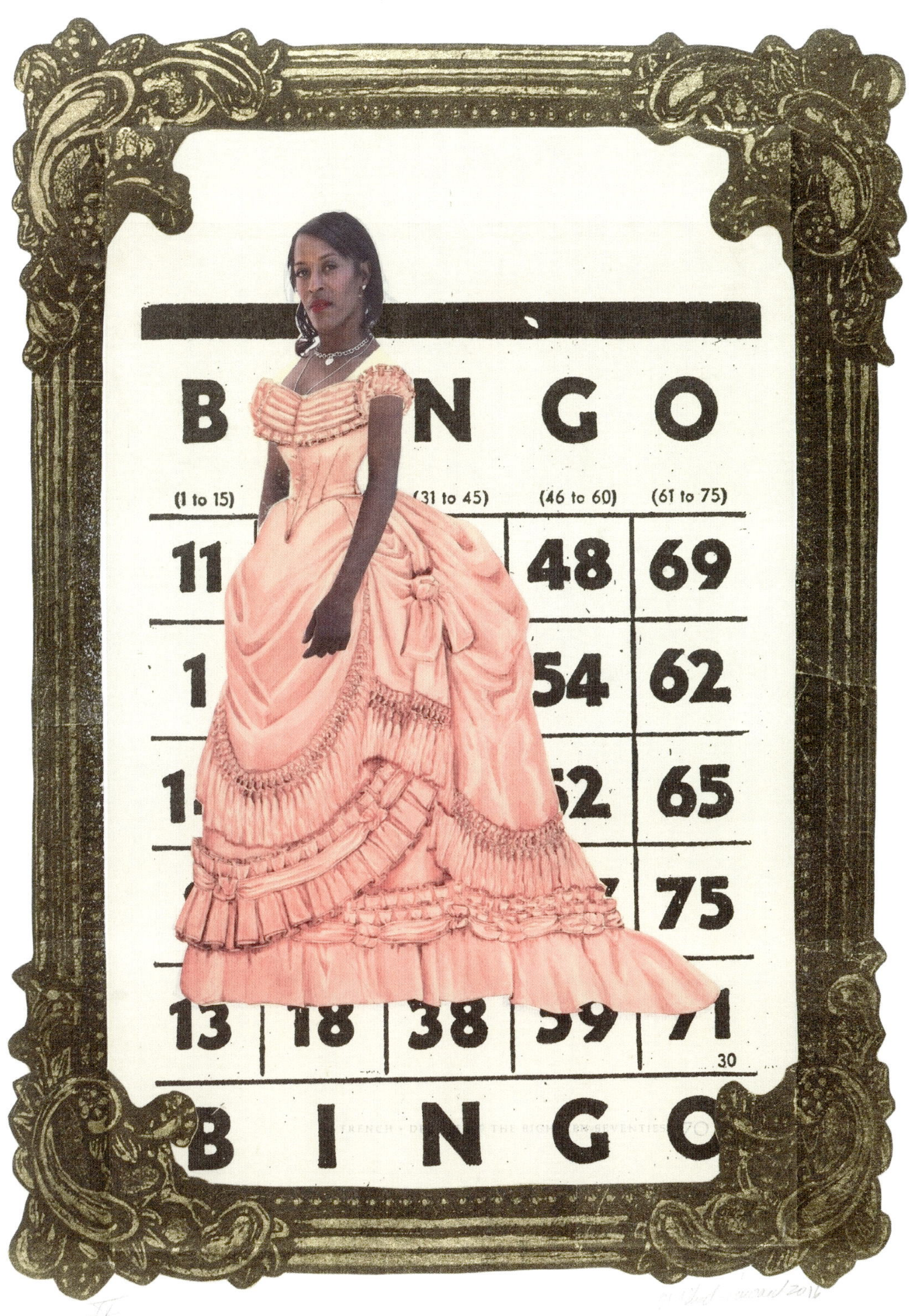
BINGO
(1 to 15)   (31 to 45)   (46 to 60)   (61 to 75)
11   48   69
1   54   62
1   52   65
75
13   18   38   59   71
30
BINGO

Wangechi Mutu (Kenyan, b. 1972), *Second Born*, 2013, 24 K gold, collagraph, relief, digital printing, collage, and hand coloring, 36 x 43 in.

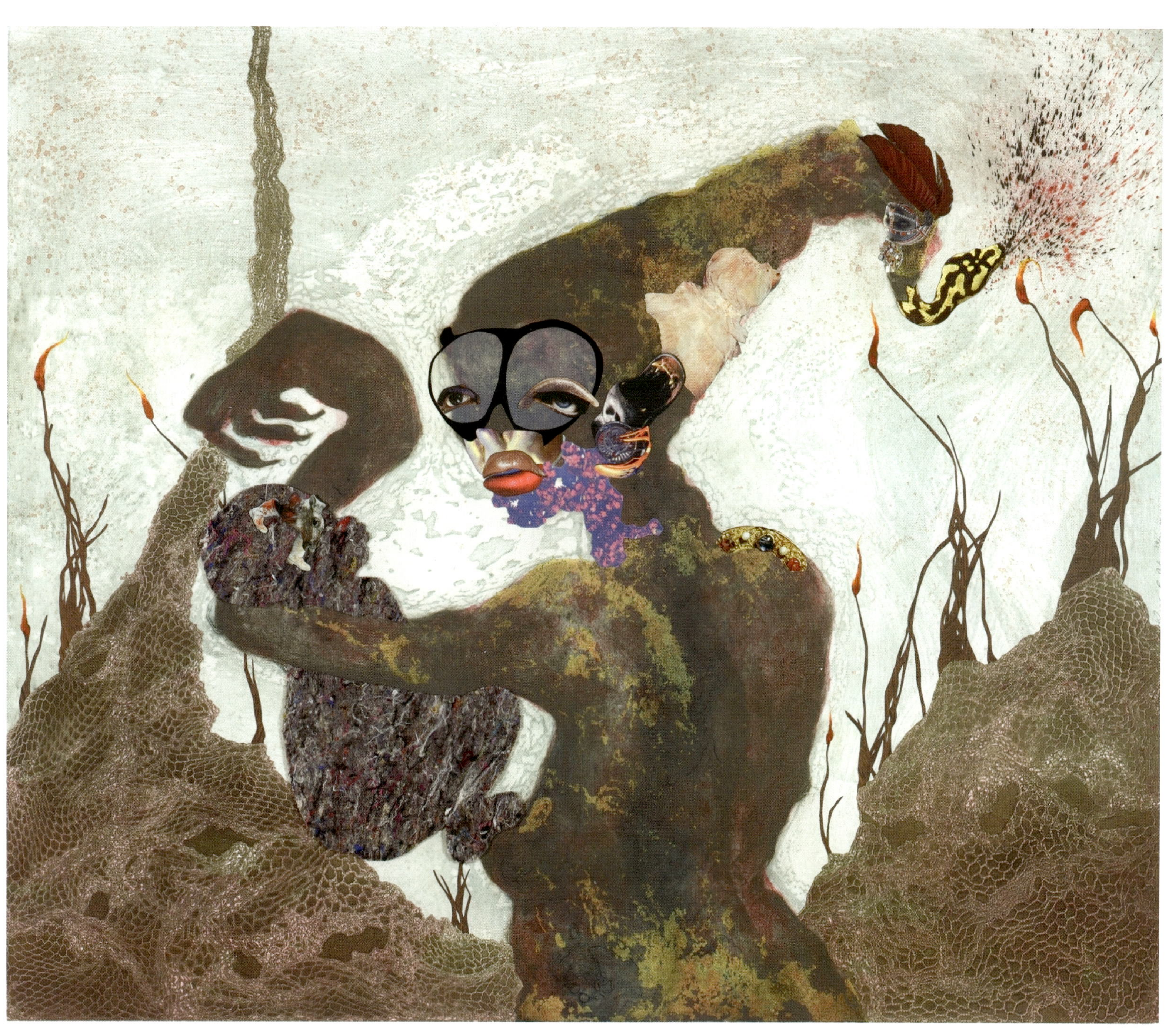

Wangechi Mutu (Kenyan, b. 1972), *Homeward Bound*, 2010, archival pigment print with screenprint in colors on archival paper, 25 x 19⅜ in.

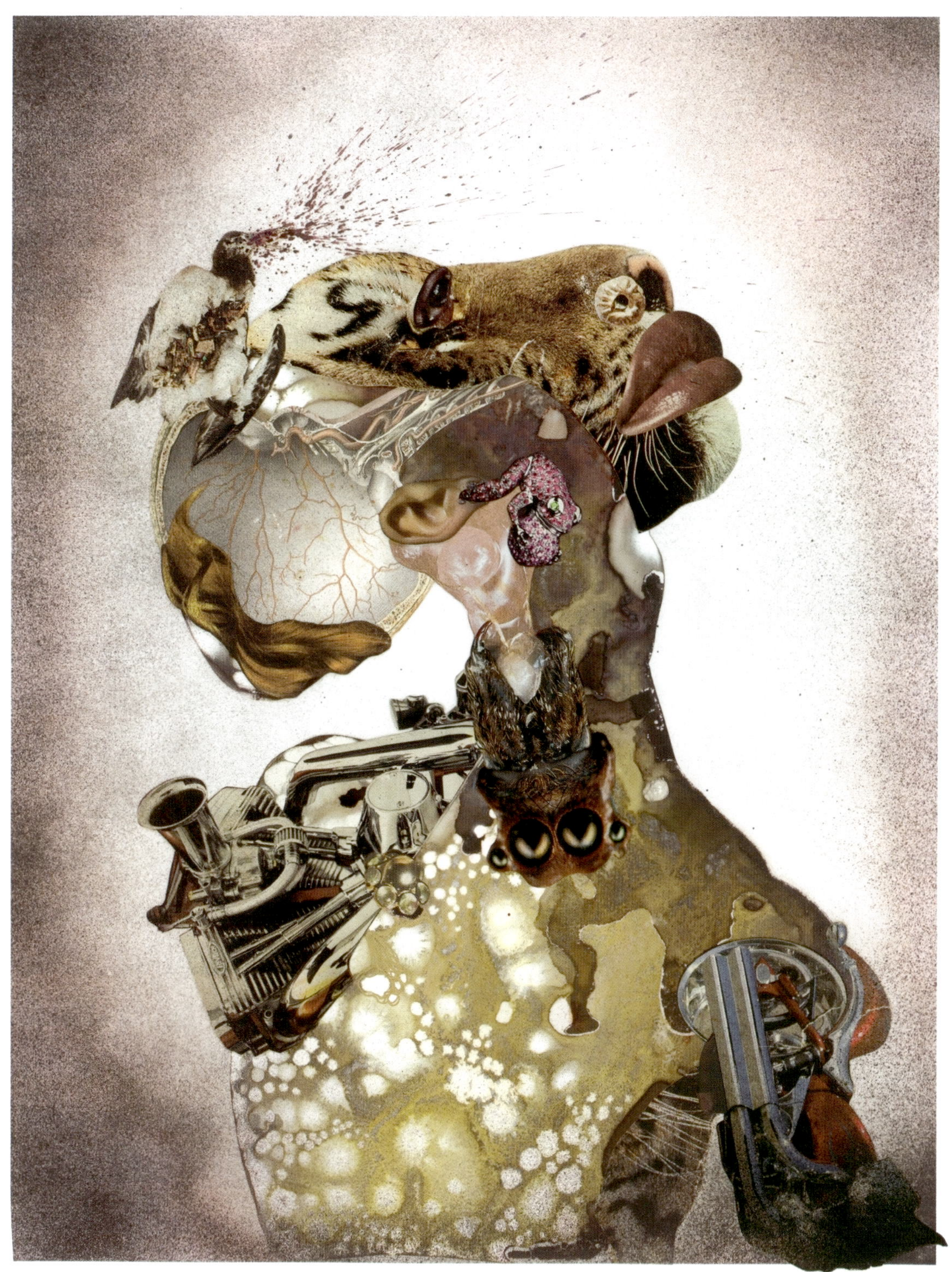

Alison Saar (American, b. 1956), *Shorn*, 2014, woodcut, 29 x 19 in.

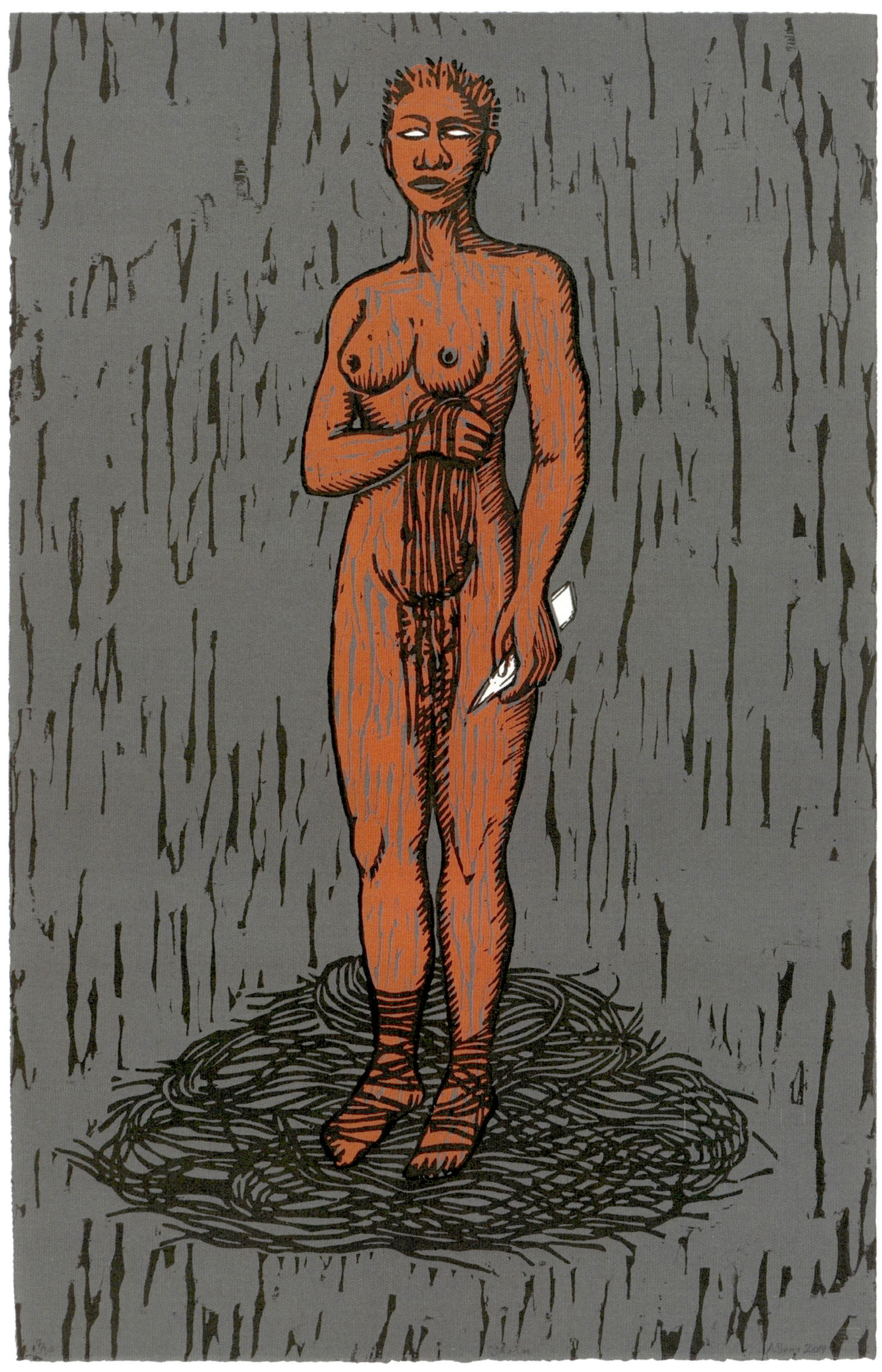

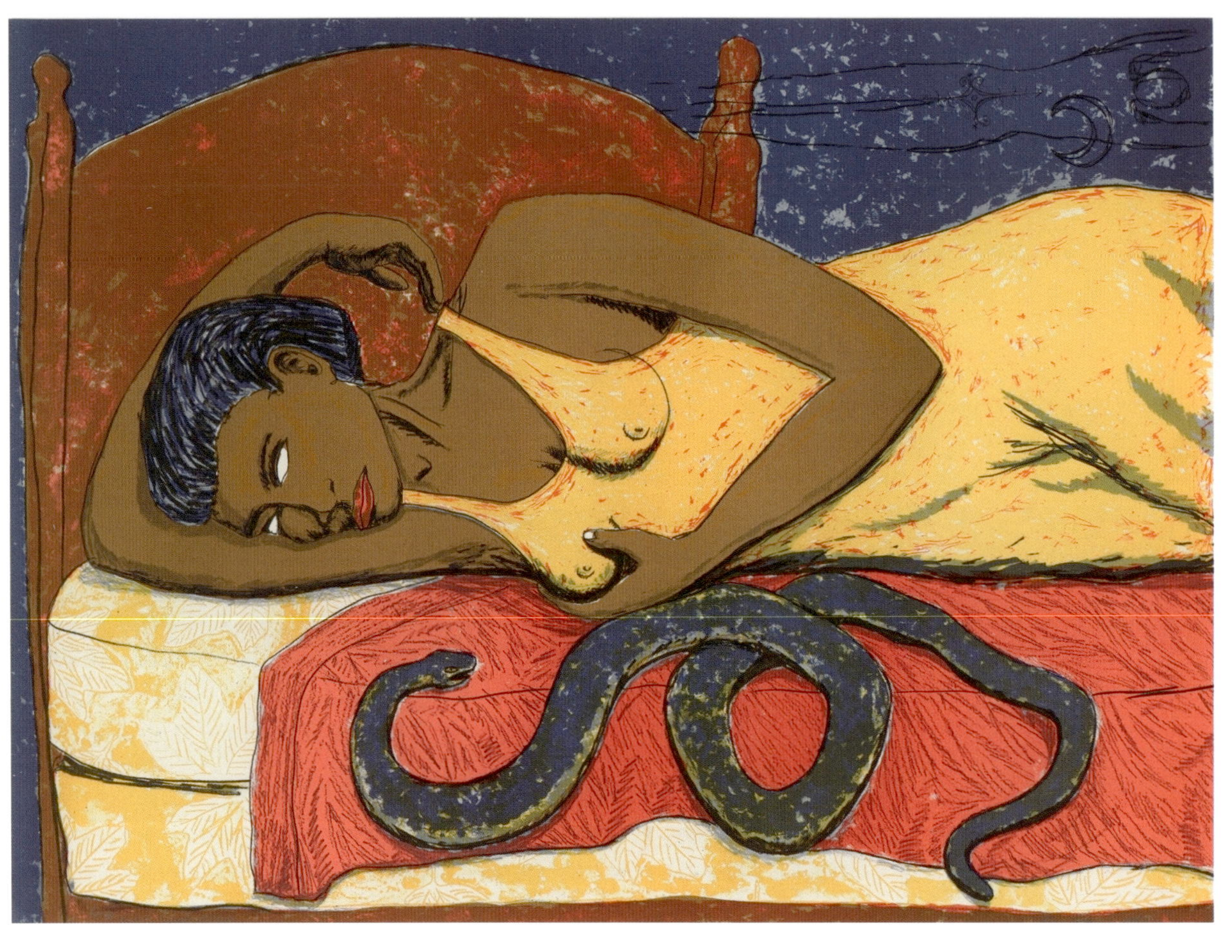

Alison Saar (American, b. 1956), *Black Snake Blues*, 1994, offset lithograph, 21¾ x 29¾ in.

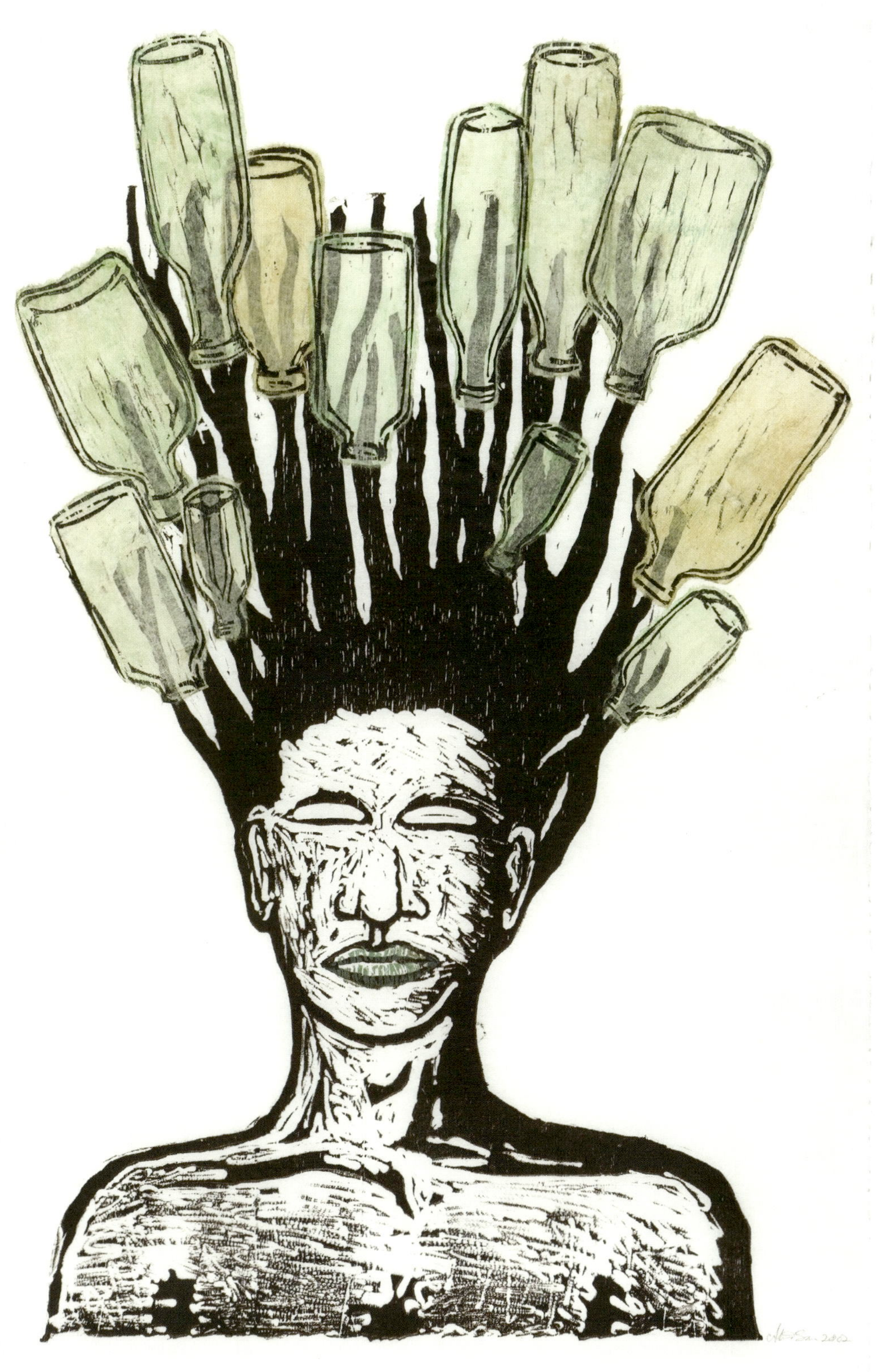

Alison Saar (American, b. 1956), *Delta Doo*, 2002, monoprint/woodcut and chine colle, 33⅞ x 24⅜ in.

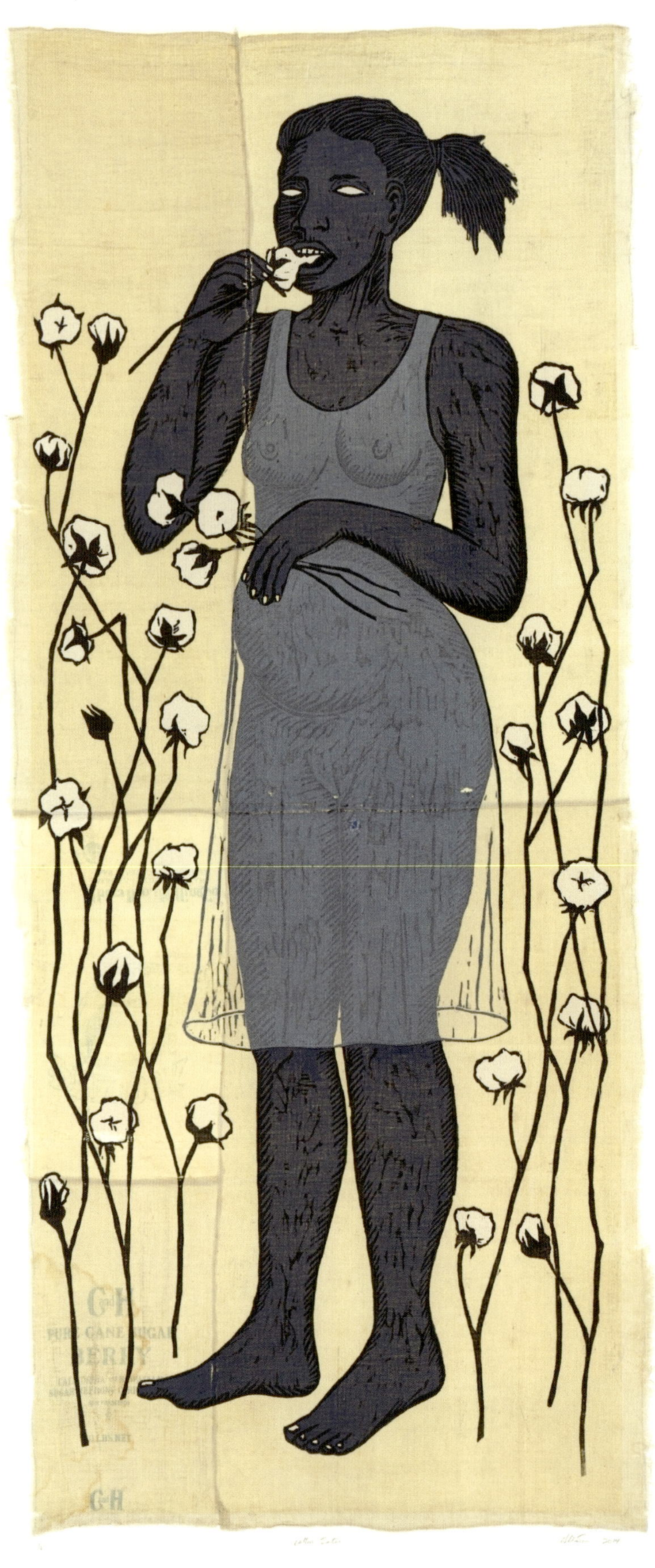

Alison Saar (American, b. 1956), *Cotton Eater*, 2014, woodcut on found sugar sack quilt, 72 x 34 in.

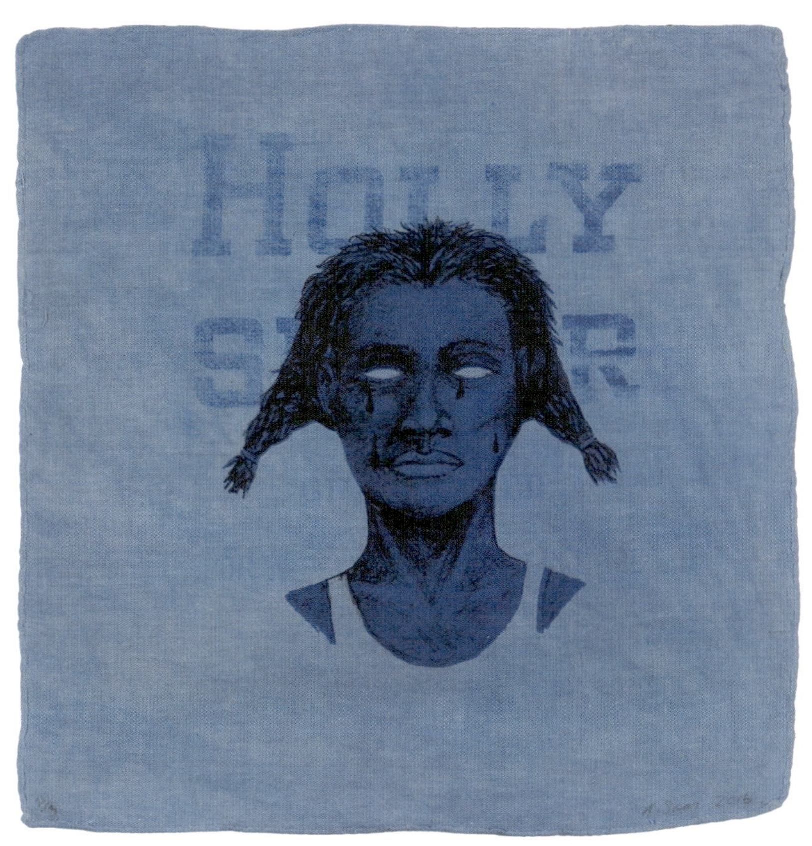

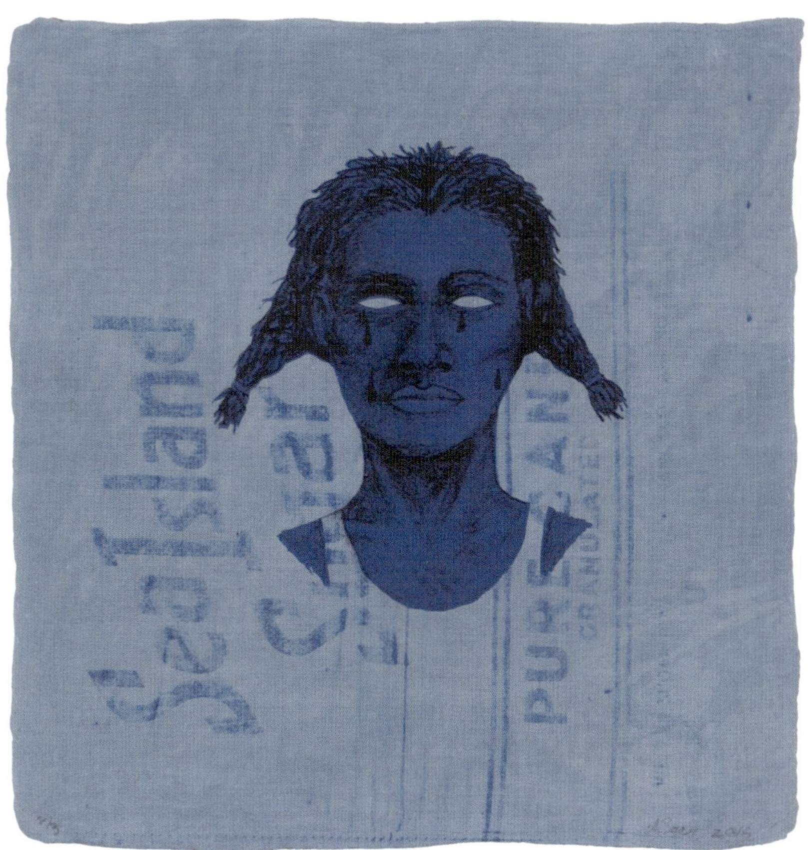

Alison Saar (American, b. 1956), *Indigo Blue (Holly Sugar)*, 2016, intaglio, 12⅛ x 12 in.
Indigo Blue (Sea Island Pure), 2016, intaglio, 12 x 11¾ in.

45

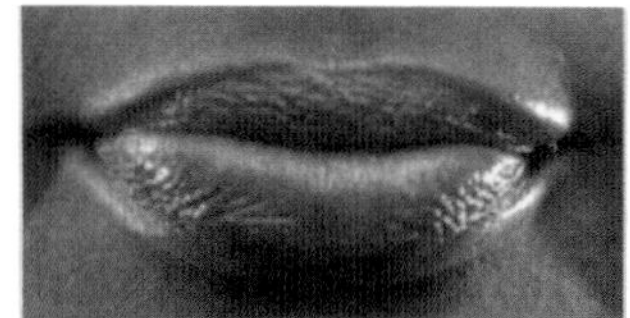

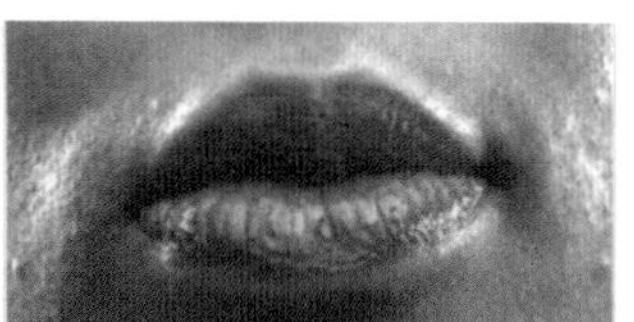

Lorna Simpson (American, b. 1960), *15 Mouths (III), (IX), (VII), and (V)*, from the portfolio *15 Mouths*, 2001–02, iris prints, each 10 x 8 in.

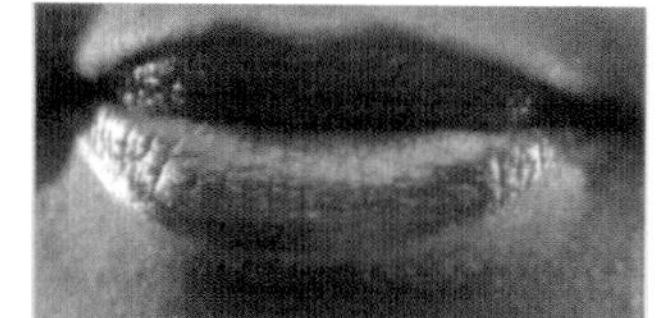

strained

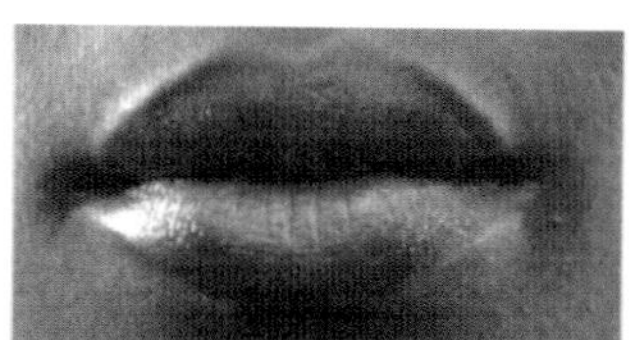

her vocal cords were overtaken by
the sound of her heartbeat

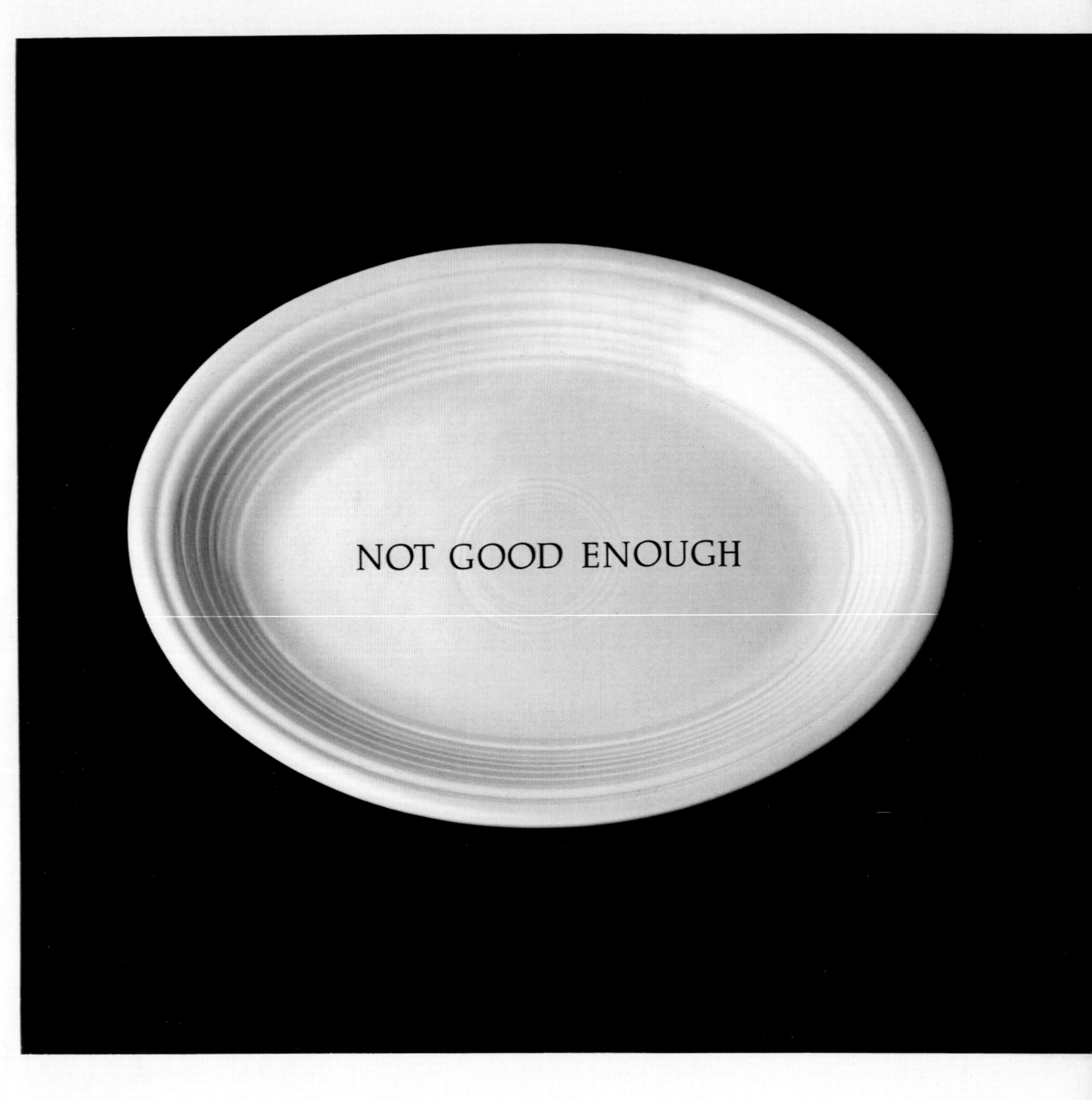

Lorna Simpson (American, b. 1960), *C-Ration*, 1991, silver gelatin print, 19 x 42 in.

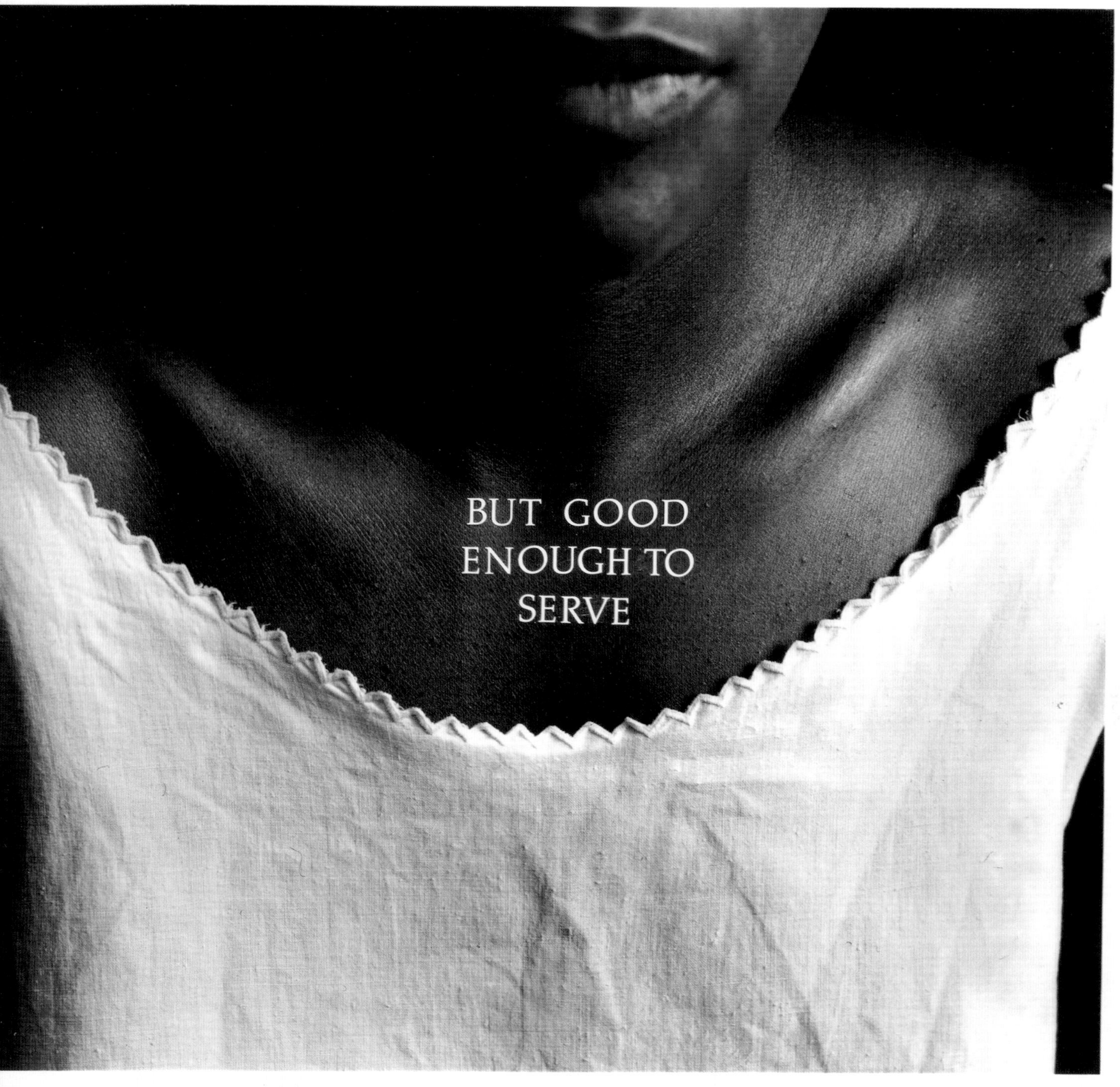
BUT GOOD
ENOUGH TO
SERVE

Mickalene Thomas (American, b. 1971), *You're Gonna Give Me the Love I Need*, 2010, collaged handmade paper with silkscreened pigmented paper pulp, pochoir, digital print, and appliqué of cloth and glitter, 24 x 30 in. © Mickalene Thomas

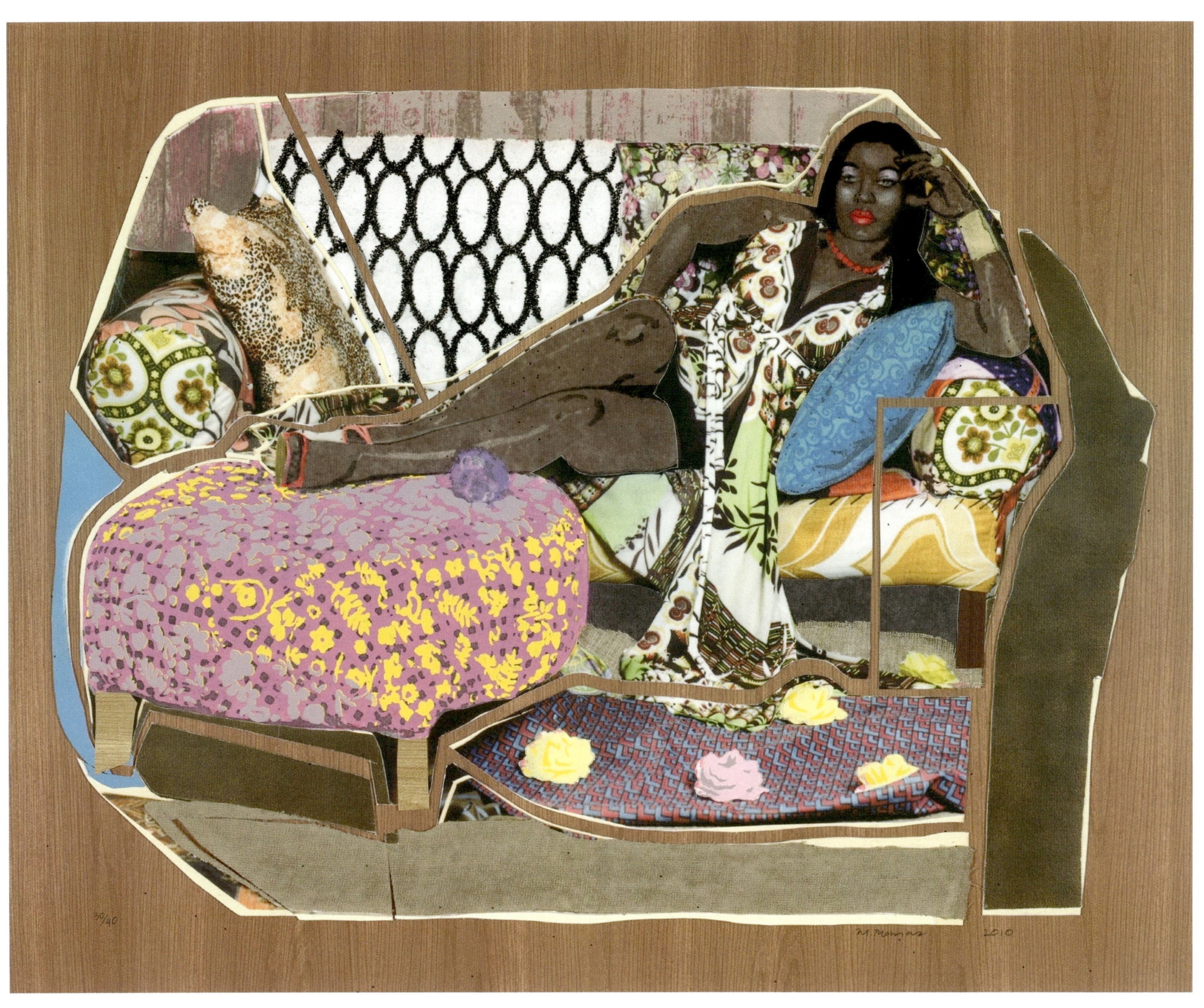

Reflections

A Conscious Musing on Body, Art, and Memory

Takiyah Nur Amin

I am most struck by visual representations that render us as we are: fully human, fully beautiful, fully vulnerable, and fully realized. While I am not a visual artist it isn't at all lost on me that the choice — because surely it is one — to present black bodies visually — and especially Black women's bodies — causes a kind of psychological and creative weight on the artist. So many negative ideas have been projected onto the physicality of Black people in general and Black women in particular that presenting us — beyond the overly determined readings of others, is a task. A worthy and necessary task taken on by the artists in this exhibit. A responsibility. A choosing. A calling.

What do I know about Black women's bodies? I know that our mere presence is often perceived as a disruption to white joy, white pleasure — saying no words and rendered mute on a canvas makes no difference. What I know is that when Black women's bodies are presented artistically beyond and outside of stereotypical depictions, many of us try hard to squeeze those images back into a narrow and archaic frame. I know that looking at stylizations of Black women's bodies here — in the fullness of their diversity — makes me feel, at least temporarily, a little more real, a little more understood, a little more actualized. Images have power… symbols call us into being.

Here we are rendered through light and shadow, color and the absence thereof. Our features are highlighted, obscured, stylized, and exaggerated. Observers of these works are beckoned to not look, but see: What memories are here? What is absent? Who is represented? What do you feel? Do you feel? Do you feel when you look at Black women's bodies? On canvas? In the world? Do our fully human selves only have value when they are one-dimensional, flattened and consumed? Or do these images call you to look beyond them, to something, to someone real?

There are things about Black women's bodies that I know… it is a deep and musky knowing from having been raised a Black girl in these United States. I know that our bodies seem to only have value when they are a commodity. I know that whenever we deploy our bodies for our own pleasure, joy, or profit, somebody somewhere is angry about it. I know that when we use our voices for our own ends the harmonies emanating from the many women inside of us are a beautiful cacophony of sound necessary for liberation. I know that once you see us, you may look away. But you will not forget.

The artists in this exhibit have taken on the task…and assumed the responsibility and psychic weight…of making legible Black women's realities. The materials, while specific, ultimately do not matter. What matters here is that we let these images linger and implicate our own bodies—How does looking at the images make us think about our own corporeal selves? We are invited here to engage the reality of our earthly, fleshy incarnation that makes each of us both magic and real.

Breathe in. Breathe out. Look. SEE.

———————————

Takiyah Nur Amin, PhD, is Assistant Professor of Dance Studies and Affiliate Faculty in the Department of Africana Studies at the University of North Carolina at Charlotte where she teaches courses in dance history and theory in the liberal studies curriculum, Department of Dance and College of Art and Architecture Honors Program. Her research and teaching interests include Black performance and aesthetics, 20th century American concert dance, and pedagogical issues in dance studies. Dr. Amin is currently working on a book project that explores the work of Black women choreographers during the height of the U.S.-based Black Power and Black Arts Movements.

Breaking Stereotypes:
Undoing Tainted Images of Black Women

Velva Boles

Being born a Black American female ignites a particularly tedious journey where stereotypes and generational obstacles have been constructed and institutionalized. The blackface minstrel shows of the 19th century portrayed Black people as naive, superstitious, and ignorant, propelling the concept of an inferiority of people of color. American society has encumbered the Black female in such a way that she must endure and succeed despite the yoke that America's legacy puts forth in the pervasive stereotypes of "mammy," "jezebel," and "Sapphire."

The *Mammy* archetype emerged from American Civil War (1861–1865) descriptions of enslaved Black household women who were depicted as being dedicated to the enslaving family, especially to the children. A *mammy* was considered by white family members as their surrogate mother and often a *mammy* was also a "wet nurse," who breast-fed and cared for the enslaver's children.

In contrast, enslaved Black women who worked in the cotton, sugar cane, tobacco, and rice fields were characterized as strong, masculine workhorses who labored with Black men in the fields, possessing aggressive, overbearing natures. The angry Black woman trope was popularized in the radio show Amos 'n' Andy, which aired in America from 1928–1960. *Sapphire* was a character designed from the enslaved field female ilk, a domineering female who emasculated men and usurped the male authority. When the show moved to television, Black actors took over the majority of the roles, which were scripted and produced by white men, and the buffoonery was exaggerated and made more widespread.

Jezebel, as described in the Hebrew Bible, fabricated evidence against an innocent landowner who refused to sell his property to her husband causing the landowner to be put to death. The name "Jezebel" became associated with "deceiver," and because the reference female wore finery and makeup there was an inclusion of women with loose behavior, prostitutes. In America, *Jezebel* embodied the European perverted idea that Black women were sexually promiscuous, evidenced by the scarcity of clothes worn by Black African people. Europeans purported that the practice of polygamy in the African culture indicated uncontrolled lust. Enslavers further distorted their observations of tribal dances as forms of sexually exciting orgies. White enslavers used the *Jezebel* image as a justification for their forced procreation among enslaved Black women; thereby legitimizing sexual assault of Black females by white males.

The legacies of "myths" describing the Black woman in the United States force us to construct a shield to protect ourselves from negativity, rise above it, and work to transform circumstances to an acceptable existence. Uncloaking is often painful so creating art is refreshing and cathartic whenever words are not enough.

Velva Boles, MD, PhD, is presently the Quality Control Director for Water Transit Solutions, a privately-owned global clean water agency domiciled in Atlanta, Georgia. Dr. Boles is a physician-scientist who practiced clinical medicine for twenty-five years after completing postgraduate training in molecular biology-gene regulation and post-medical residency at Tulane Medical Center. Dr. Boles was a Visiting Researcher at the Center for Disease Control Zoonotic Division in Fort Collins, Colorado, investigating Hanta Virus, Lyme Disease, and Dengue Fever mechanisms of infection and virulence. As a consultant, Dr. Boles has executed the duties of Laboratory Medical Director for an international immunohematochemical corporation, earning CLIA certification as was required to establish and maintain quality standards specified by the Food and Drug Administration and European Medical Agency. Dr. Boles has published three white papers, numerous healthcare blogs and articles, and presented more than 200 invited orations and technical papers on disparity of healthcare for Black Americans.. Dr. Boles is also a diplomat of the American College of Forensic Examiners.

African American Women Artists' Magical Truths

Claire Oberon Garcia

*Art allows you to imbue the truth with a sort of magic… so it can infiltrate the psyches of
more people, including those who don't believe the same things as you.*

— WANGECHI MUTU

The lived experiences of Black women in the United States are varied and complicated, shaped by creative responses to the restrictions that a white supremacist, patriarchal society still tries to impose on its citizens. The most likely person to read a book — in any format — is a Black woman who's been to college.[1] In 2012, seventy-four percent of Black women in the U.S. eligible to vote exercised this fundamental citizenship right, reflecting their long tradition of higher rates of voter participation than any other demographic. Yet Black women continue to be underrepresented at all levels of local, state, and national government.

African American women hold more than half of all science and engineering degrees completed by Black people and start their own businesses at a rate six times higher than the national average, yet Black women in the U.S. earn less than white women doing full-time, year-round work, regardless of educational level.

Hypertension and other stress-related diseases are more common among African American women than any other group, and although white women have higher rates of breast cancer, Black women are more likely to die of the disease.

In the more than 400 years of being here in this country, Black women artists and activists have been resisting the controlling images that ignore Black women's subjectivity and agency, past and present. U.S. culture's controlling images — from Jezebel to the Strong Black Woman — have shaped and even extinguished Black women's lives, yet Black artists have always interrogated the historical and ideological narratives that sought to reduce and dismiss Black women's humanity.

---

1 http://www.pewinternet.org/2014/01/16/e-reading-rises-as-device-ownership-jumps/

I see the work of each of the artists represented here as interrogating how identities are formed: how they are shaped and inflected by cultural and historical discourses; how the intersections of race, gender, sexuality, and other axes of difference play out at a time (post-modernity) in which identities are fluid and mutable; and how art, through the power of different media and materials, both reflects and creates ways of knowing and understanding the world.

Each of these artists selects images from historical, personal, popular culture and contemporary palettes to meditate on the variety of Black women's being: as figures in ethnographic or religious narratives, as artificers of their own realms, whether that realm is the family or the stage or the imagination, and as citizens or outsiders in narratives of national and gender identities. These pieces invite the viewer to think about the processes, both material and immaterial, of image making and identity.

Claire Oberon Garcia is a professor of English, and the director of Race, Ethnicity, and Migration Studies at Colorado College.

Poetry of Process

Jean Gumpper and Kate Leonard

Artworks in *Beyond Mamie, Jezebel & Sapphire: Reclaiming Images of Black Women* explore printmaking's long relationship with social justice themes. They also encourage us to consider how the juxtaposition of particular printmaking techniques can be used to articulate relationships of power and how the marks and processes used by African American women artists can reclaim their imagery.

Cutting, carving, and stamping are physical and visceral movements of our daily lives and are an integral part of the vocabulary of printmaking. From the etchings of Ellen Gallagher to the photo/letterpress works of Lorna Simpson, the cogency between content and process is ever present. In *Shorn*, Alison Saar presents a central female figure that has cut her own hair with a shard of glass. Saar actualizes the intensity and physicality of this image by choosing woodcut as her process. As viewers, we are able to trace her carving tools through the wood, following a rain of cut marks across the surface that gather with shorn hair piled at the figure's feet. Not only do we explicitly understand the image of the defiant woman holding a glass shard, we implicitly understand the image of artist Alison Saar as she physically carves with her razor-sharp tools. While working with printers at Tandem Press at the University of Wisconsin, Saar also leads printers and assistants to produce works like this and other printed works.

Screen print and offset lithography are processes that invite the use of found imagery, collage, and stencils. Wangechi Mutu's series *Histology of the Different Classes of Uterine Tumors* was produced at Hare & Hound Press in San Antonio. Offset lithography was used to translate her powerful collages of fragile and fugitive medical illustrations into permanent archival multiples. After printing, Mutu directed the printers to apply glittered handwork on top of the commercial offset layer, forcing a conversation between two very different types of processes, one personal and one commercial, a juxtaposition that echoes the questions of constructed identity raised in the imagery itself. Similarly, in Kara Walker's series *Harper's Pictorial History of the Civil War,* Walker screen printed her meticulously hand-cut stencil silhouettes on top of offset lithographs of historical engravings. Throughout each print,

Walker masterfully controls the dialogue between silkscreen silhouette and offset litho. In *Exodus of Confederates from Atlanta*, Walker's dominant female silhouette sits on top of the narrative scene and pushes past the edges of the frame to assert her voice as the last word in the conversation between these two distinct layers.

Reading the marks and layers of these prints and understanding the artist in the printshop, we are able to experience the intense physicality of these images in a very different way than if they were drawn with pencil or painted with a brush.

Professors **Jean Gumpper** and **Kate Leonard** teach printmaking and drawing at Colorado College. Professor Leonard is an etcher who directs the Graphics Research Lab, an innovative printmaking and design program. Professor Gumpper specializes in color reduction woodcuts. Both exhibit their print work nationally and internationally.

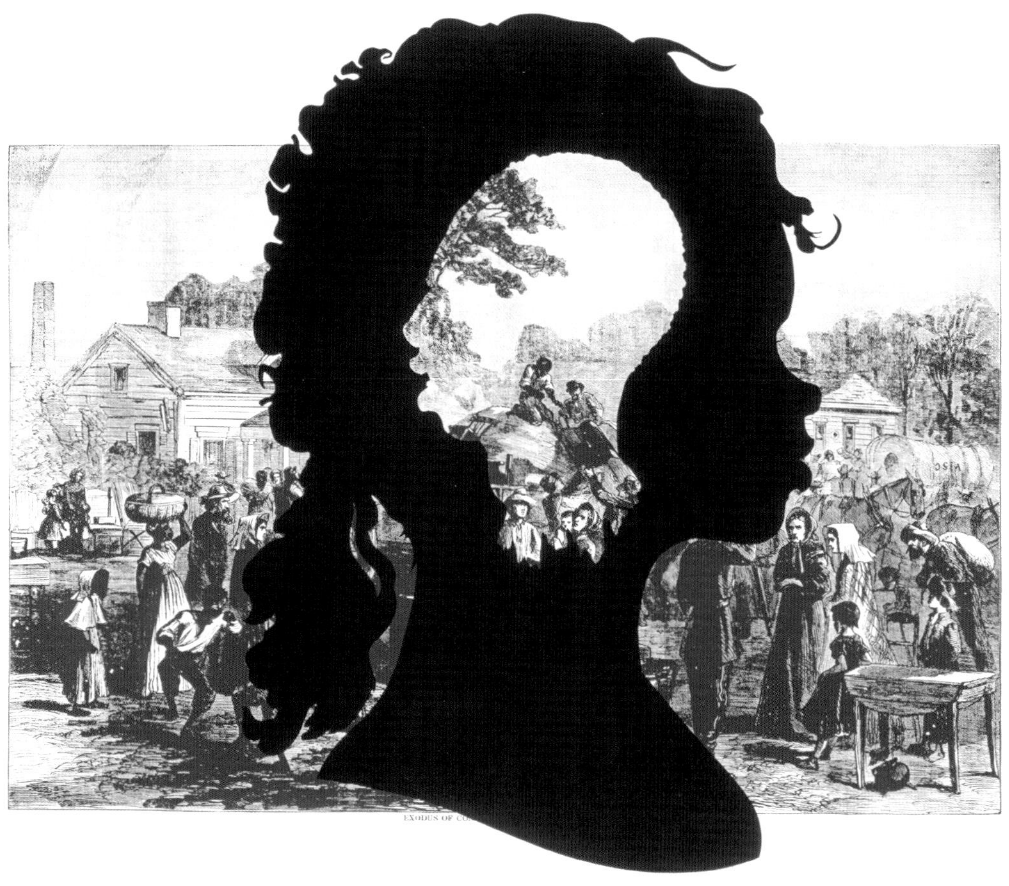

Kara Walker (American, b. 1969), *Harper's Pictorial History of the Civil War (Annotated): Exodus of Confederates from Atlanta*, 2005, offset lithography and screenprint, 39 x 53 in. ©Kara Walker, courtesy of Sikkema Jenkins & Co., New York.

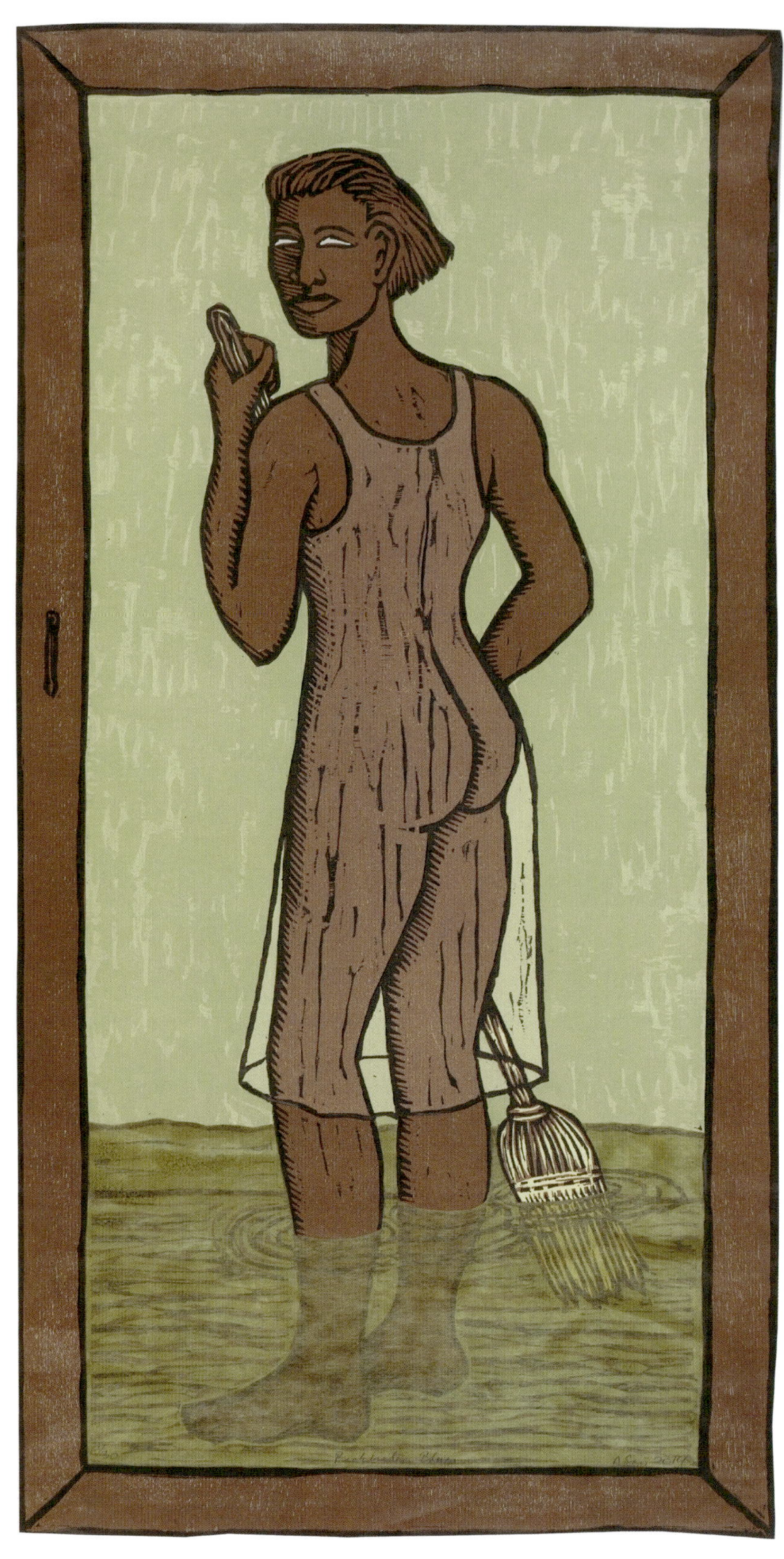

Alison Saar (American, b. 1956), *Backwater Blues*, 2014, woodcut, fabric dye, shellac, shine appliqué, 27⅜ x 14⅜ in.

Lifting the Veil and Reclaiming
Black Women's Humanity

Venetria K. Patton

Beyond Mammy, Jezebel & Sapphire: Reclaiming Images of Black Women is a powerful exhibit that looks beneath the veil of images obstructing our true view of Black womanhood. Alison Saar's *Backwater Blues, edition 2/30*, of 2014, strikes me as an apropos metaphor for the exhibit. The woman in the picture is wearing a see-through dress, which reveals both her nakedness and her vulnerability. In many ways, the images gathered in this exhibit allow participants to look beneath the stereotype of the strong Black woman and see her vulnerability, whether it be the assault on her psyche due to ideals of beauty that she can never meet, or the painful history of slavery, which still impacts her and our society.

The impact of racialized beauty ideals is particularly apparent in Robert H. Colescott's *Lock and Key II, edition 1/15*, 1989. The picture depicts a nude Black man chained to a nude white woman. The chaining points to the imprisoning effect of societal notions of racialized beauty. The man and woman both seem to be implicated, as the woman is chained by her wrists and the man by his neck. The mutuality of their imprisonment is reflected in the way in which their heads almost come together as one, with half being the black man's and the other the white woman's. The image, much like Bruce Nugent's Drawings for Mulattoes Series, calls into question our racialized distinctions. Another powerful image, which also addresses the impact of racialized beauty ideals, is Wangechi Mutu's *Histology of the Different Classes of Uterine Tumors: Adult Female Sexual Organs, edition 14/25*, 2006. In this collage, Mutu depicts the devastating effects of these ideals through the metaphor of disease. The woman's head is essentially a massive tumor and at the center is the idealized white woman, in stark contrast to her dark skin and thick lips.

Mutu's collage is riveting because the eyes appear to be tearing up in acknowledgement of the woman's pain while still attempting to remain steadfast and stoic. This is the dilemma of the strong Black woman: she is not to know or show pain, yet holding it in, as the subject of Mutu's collage has done, will only lead to disease. Mutu depicts the disease with white fur, reminiscent of cotton. Cotton and the history of slavery haunt this exhibit. Even more playful images such as Mildred Howard's I've Been a Witness to this Game Series call attention to the painful legacy of colonialism and slavery. The first image from the series features a digital image of Beyoncé in the forefront of an army battalion, suggesting that Black women are in formation. The other images of the series call attention to colonialism and slavery, but the women are not bent or bowed down because they've seen this game before—in other words, Howard pays tribute to the strength of Black women despite adversity. Thus the exhibition does not deny Black women's strength and resiliency, but puts it into context by also endowing Black women with human frailty—we are strong Black women, not superhuman—and we feel a broad range of human emotions including: pain, anguish, fear, tenderness, sassiness, pleasure, and joy. By reclaiming the image of Black women, this exhibit insists on our multidimensional humanity.

PAGE 65–67: **Wangechi Mutu** (Kenyan, b. 1972), *Histology of the Different Classes of Uterine Tumors,* 2006, glitter, ink, collage on found medical illustration paper, each 23 x 17 in.

———————

Venetria K. Patton, PhD, is Director of the African American Studies and Research Center and Professor of English, Purdue University.

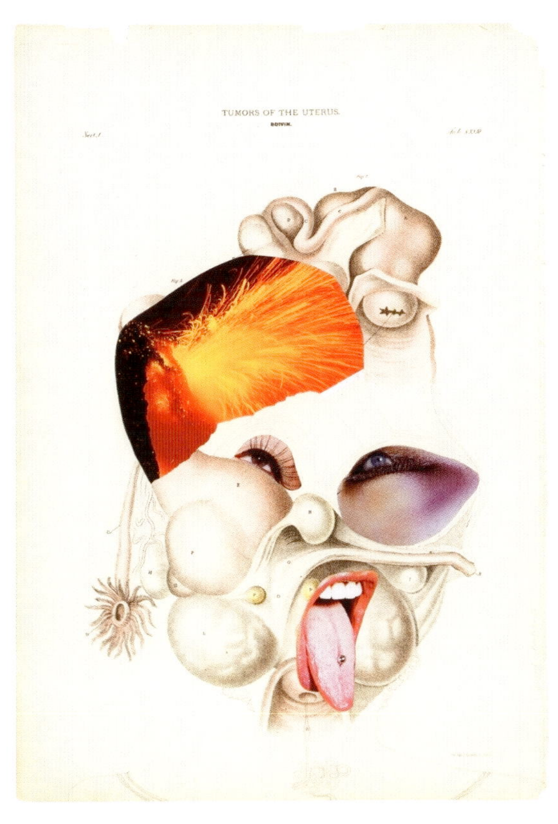

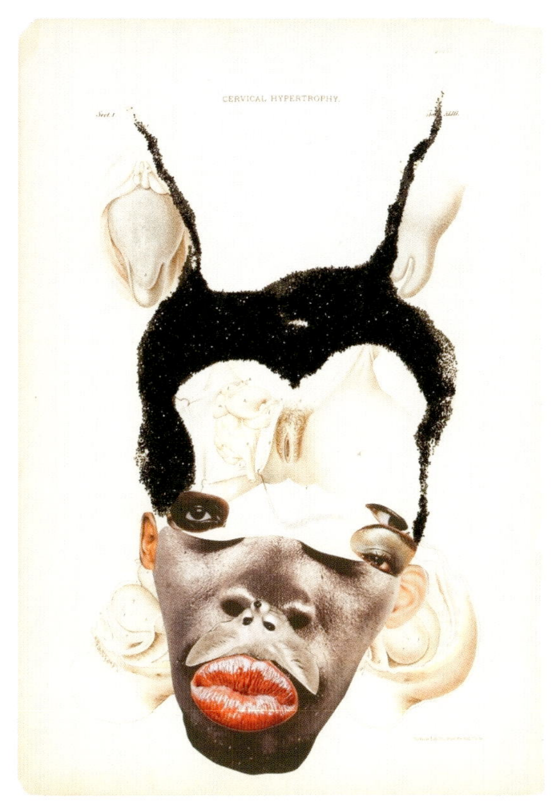

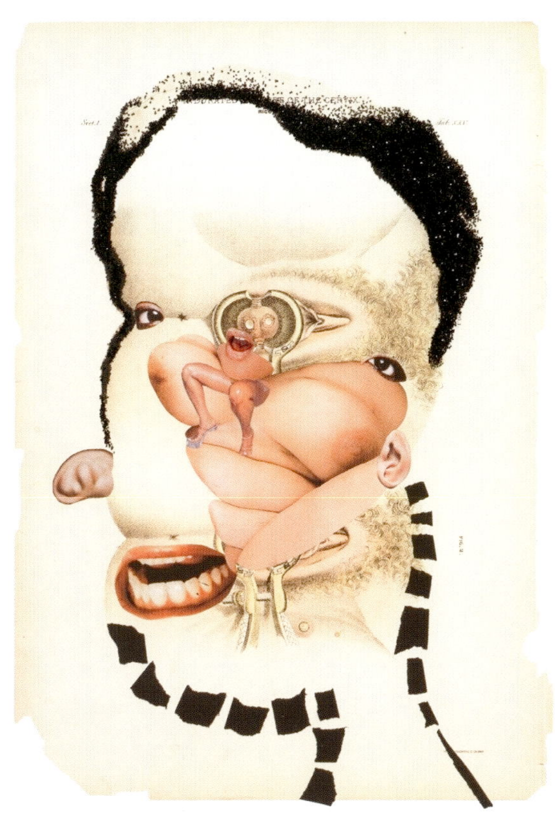

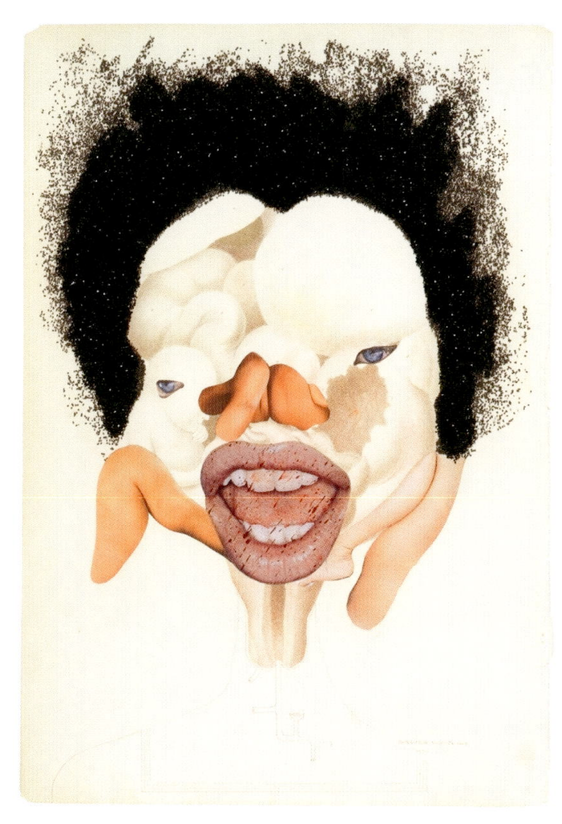

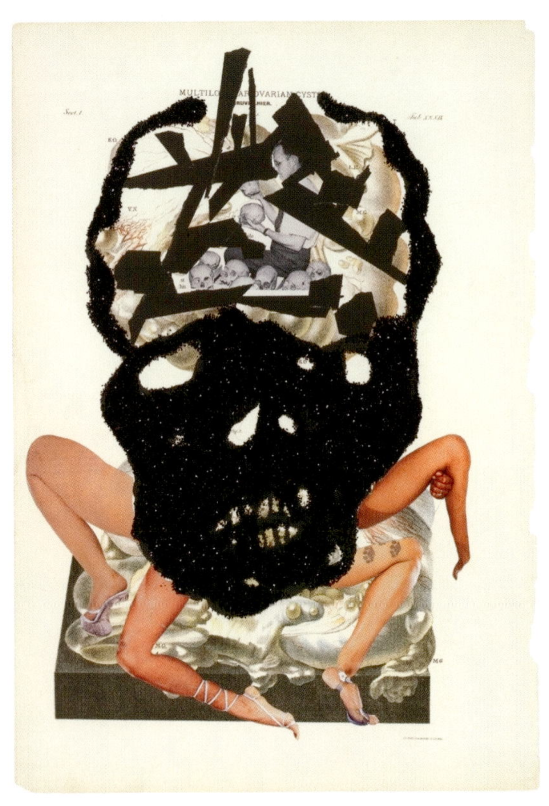
MULTILOCULAR OVARIAN CYST

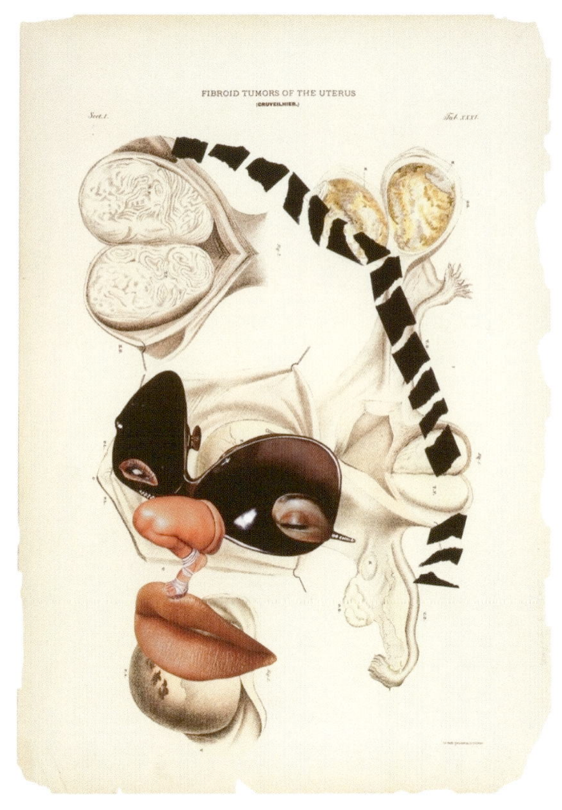
FIBROID TUMORS OF THE UTERUS

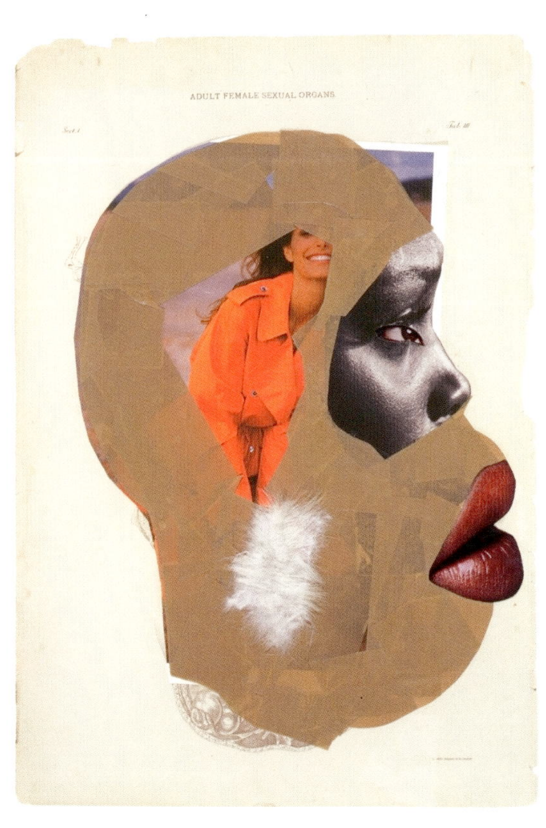
ADULT FEMALE SEXUAL ORGANS

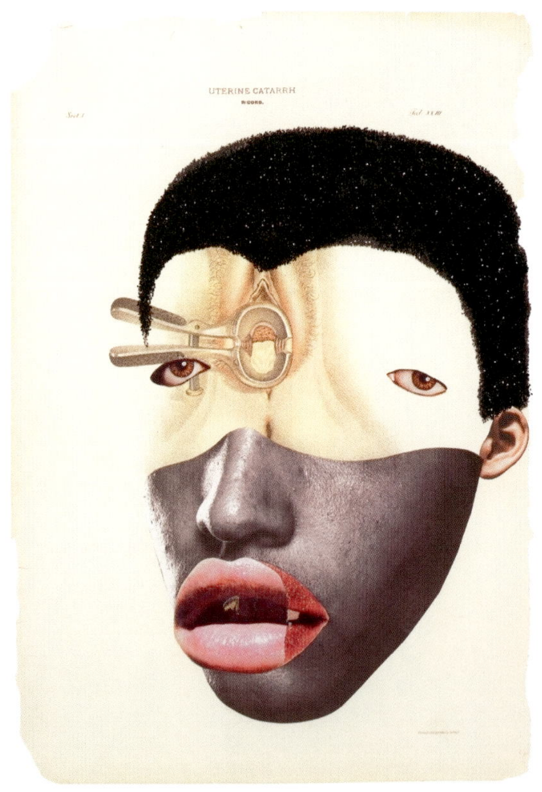
UTERINE CATARRH

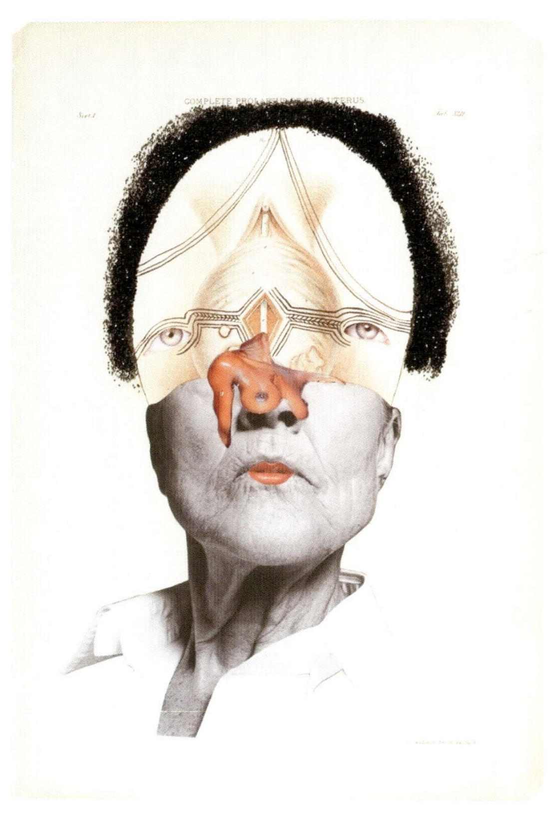
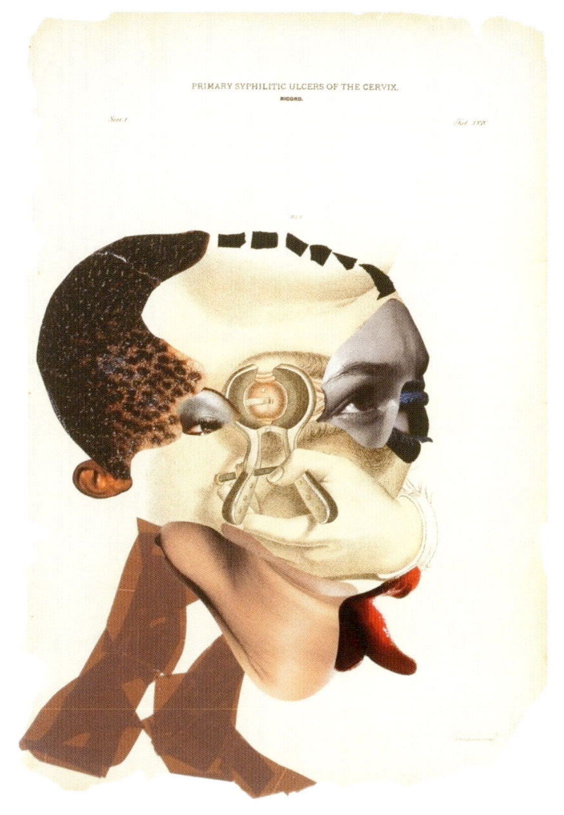
PRIMARY SYPHILITIC ULCERS OF THE CERVIX.
RICORD.
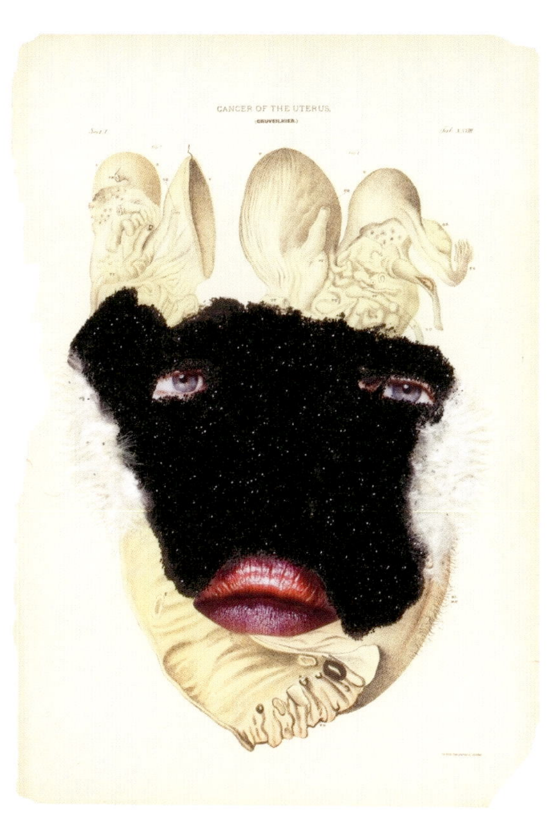
CANCER OF THE UTERUS.
(CRUVEILHIER.)
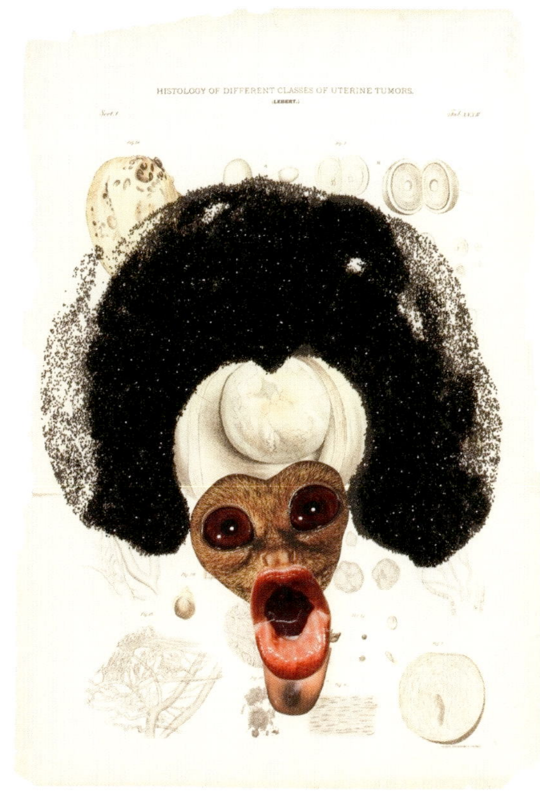
HISTOLOGY OF DIFFERENT CLASSES OF UTERINE TUMORS.
(LEBERT.)

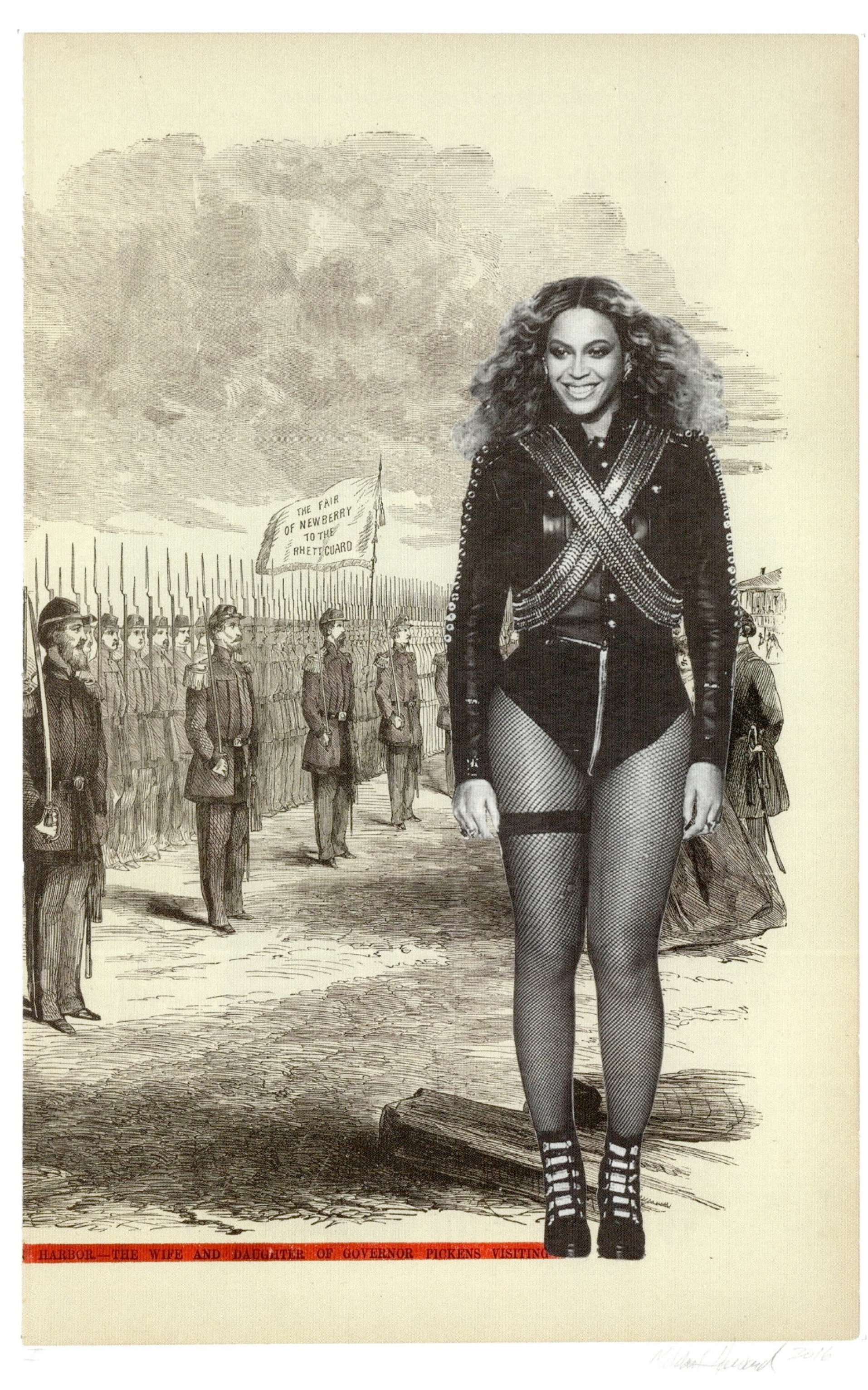

Mildred Howard (American, b. 1945), *I've Been a Witness to this Game I*, 2016, color monoprint/digital on found paper with collage, 20⅝ x 15⅛ in.

Taking Back Me
(for Beyond Mammy, Jezebel, and Sapphire)

by Sha'Condria "iCon" Sibley

This is me coming back for what is mine.
This is me standing in the vast, white fields of your oppression
and picking all of my body parts
and bones
off the bushels of your tongue
and stuffing them into my cotton satchel.
This time, *I* will do the weighing,
which is to say,
this time, I will determine my own worth.
I am more than your numbers
and nicknames
and negative images,
where you have painted me in vibrantly grotesque shades
of mammy, villain, and vixen.
This is me showing you my true colors.
Ain't gon be no more Aunt Jemima's spilling sweet syrup from our lips,
calling you "Master" and "Mistress"
when it tastes more like leftover scraps
from meals my hands have made.
You won't be picking any pickannies off auction blocks
to raise your stock
or play ragdoll for your spoiled children.
We are tired of playing your childish games.
Miss Mary Mack Mack Mack
all dressed in black
face and placed on stage for your entertainment.
No more tap-dancing, lap-dancing for your dollar bills.
You can't buy sex that ain't for sale.
I have never been for sale.
When you arrived on my continent,
came uninvited to the party,
and saw me in the body that God had given to me,
moving that same body to a rhythm

that He failed to give to you,
you mistook praise for promiscuity.
Saw my wide hips as open door.
Big breasts as open feast
for your famine.
This time, I will command my milk to dry up
when it hears your panting like a thirsty dog in heat.
I will howl at the moon
and summon all the bad bitches to shed our fur
and show you the black girl magic underneath.
Show you how we both cast *and* break spells.
With one pat of my 'fro,
one bounce of my curls,
one flip of my bangs,
one twist of my locs,
how we can remove the ones you've placed on us.
Show you how my identity don't belong in cages,
how my femininity comes in all different stages.
Show you how this black womanhood is both body
and bigger than body
at the same damn time.
And I hope you hear me loud and clear,
because this message is being brought to you live
and in stereotypes
that are meant to be broken
like the system that created them.
This is me breaking
what never should have been built in the first place.
Taking back
what never should have been stolen.

© Sha'Condria "iCon" Sibley, 2016.

Sha'Condria "iCon" Sibley is a nationally acclaimed championship poet/spoken word artist/multidisciplinary performer/teaching artist. Her work has been featured on many national and international outlets such as Huffington Post, For Harriet, Fusion, *Marie Claire*, *Teen Vogue*, *In Style* magazine, and she even made BET's 2015 list of Black Girls Winning. She was a featured performer on the third season of TV One's Verses and Flow. A two-time national slam champion, iCon also became the first woman and non-Texan to win the Texas Grand Slam, the largest individual poetry slam in the South, in 2015. She was also the inaugural 2015 Rouge Roulette Slam Champion and currently ranks as the #2 female poet in the world. Most recently, she and her slam team, Team SNO (Slam New Orleans) won the 2016 Southern Fried Regional Poetry Slam, the second largest team slam in the nation, and became the first poetry act ever to grace the main stage at the 2016 Essence Festival. In addition to her accomplishments, iCon has starred in many stage plays and works teaching poetry to inmates at a federal correctional facility. She is the host and organizer of the Rhythm & Rhymes Spoken Word Performing Arts Series at the Alexandria Museum of Art and founder of the Little Girls Big Names Project.

Fragments of a Piece

Karen Riley Simmons

Self-sacrificing Mammy. Promiscuous Jezebel. Angry Sapphire. I am well acquainted with this triad of stereotypes, commonly ascribed to my Black sisters and me. The nature of stereotypes is, they narrow the view and distort the viewer's perception of the subject. Sometimes I recognize that narrowed view, directed toward me in the filtered gaze of others —when dressed smartly in street clothes, I'm mistaken as the server or the stock clerk, or ignored when in line to be served.

The distorted gaze assails me daily, projected through movies, music, advertising, and other media. Producers exploit the Jezebel image with so-called video vixens. Some reality television franchises could well be dubbed "The Real Sapphires," as they brazenly capitalize on backbiting, catfights, and rancor.

Occasionally, I even glimpse the trio in the mirror. Mammy admonishes, "You're not going to *wear* those leggings, are you?" Sapphire frowns when I start applying eyeliner. Jezebel gives me the side-eye if I don't. Other times, I hear their murmurs in my head. As my mother's caretaker and the mother of a young adult making her way in the world, Mammy demands a lot and delivers a load of guilt. Sapphire harangues me for not living up to my "potential" as writer, while Jezebel lures me to online dating sites since, she says, I'm not getting any younger.

As I navigate my way forward, sixteen years since the divorce, eleven since hurricane Katrina, sometimes I feel them clutching at my heels. Rarely does one show up without the others. They are sisters of a sort, joined at the hip, a gang of bullies. Sometimes, like a towering totem, they present themselves as one, masquerading in the visage of the Strong Black Woman. It's a seductive dance they do, one that raves of self-sufficiency and strength. But it's a farce. The self-sufficiency they boast is a sham and the strength an illusion.

I have to be watchful, for it's risky to mistake any or all of these images as myself. I have to remember, as with all stereotypes, they are mere fragments of a piece and it's dangerous to view myself or my sisters through those fractured lenses.

In "ego tripping," poet Nikki Giovanni celebrates the black earth-mother-creator-goddess-queen—fully integrated, human, divine, and extraordinary in her being. She is sensual, not salacious; strong, not hard; nurturing, not self-sacrificing. I have to remind myself, not only is the Strong Black Woman dead, and her ostentatious crew with her, she never lived. Free of the weight of them, their gaze, and their whispers, like Nikki, I remember, "I can fly like a bird in the sky."

———————

Karen Riley Simmons is a writer, actor, vocalist, and arts advocate who moonlights as the creative marketing maven at KRS Kreative Write Edit Design. A native of New Orleans, she tweets about the central Louisiana arts and threatre scene as Gumbeaux Arts and is founding president of Sankofa Cultural Collective in Alexandria, Louisiana.

Beyond Mammy, Jezebel & Sapphire: Reclaiming Images of Black Women

A Black-Girl-Woman Reflection

Claudine Taaffe

In individual and collective, public and private spaces, Black women are constantly negotiating, resisting and (re)constructing narratives for the dual purpose of survival and integrity. Whether confined to an inhumane enslavement or suffocated within the stereotype of a loud Black girl, an inherent part of a Black woman's survival is to unapologetically and fearlessly resist the negative labels that are metaphorically inscribed onto our physical bodies as a result of socially constructed images about our histories, ways of being, and aspirations. Within our acts of resisting stereotypes, Black women create new and necessary locations for (re)membering, creating knowledge and art, and speaking back for not only Black women, but Black girls as well. Using artistic modes of expression is a crucial labor Black artists have historically employed for making sense of the world around us and to deconstruct the myths that dangerously suffocate the delicious fullness of who we are as Black women and girls. A significant contribution of the Black-woman centered, artistic installation, *Beyond Mammy, Jezebel & Sapphire: Reclaiming Images of Black Women*, is a demonstration of the blurring of boundaries between art and artist, stereotype and counter-narrative, theory and method, and freedom and (un)free. The encounter of the exhibit images by the observer compels an examination of the extent of dialogical transformation that occurs when Black woman-centered art is included in both physical and ethereal spaces of Black woman-dialogue for the purpose of crafting counter-stories to the dangerous binaries inherent in the "Strong Black Woman" trope. These incredible and tantalizing Black-woman centered art pieces aim to not only interrupt and transcend historical and contemporary stereotypes about Black women, but also the physical presence and boundaries of the individual artists, as their works live beyond the beautifully painful and political moments in which they were created.

This exhibit is ultimately a call to action for the lives of Black women and girls to be freed from the imperial gazes that do not allow our full selves to exist perfectly and imperfectly. In the experiencing of *Beyond Mammy, Jezebel & Sapphire*, a vulnerable journey is strategically and beautifully crafted through which the observer engages with the artists in an exchange about what it means to simultaneously be master of a labor that feeds a nation, futuristically positioned within a racialized history of sexuality, a loud and silver-lipped wordsmith, a doula of fibroids AND Black woman. What will always surface in the creation of, and engagement with, these images are the stories we remain committed to about each other, about Black women and girls, and about ourselves. In the purposeful reclaiming of images about Black women, the act is about more than simply "taking back" disconcerting images that have been used against us. It is also not about simply shifting the gaze of Black women to the center from the margins. *Beyond Mammy, Jezebel & Sapphire* is an installation of artistic creations that plays an integral role in our (re)imagining of spaces of freedom for Black women and girls — spaces where we are no longer interested in the reproduction of the inequalities that position the center and margins, binaries, and the "Strong Black Woman" trope in the first place.

Claudine Taaffe (b. 1968) is a Senior Lecturer in the African American and Diasporic Studies Program at Vanderbilt University. Taaffe received her doctorate in education from the University of Illinois. Her research is centered in examining the ways in which Black girls, who are constructed as "at-risk," negotiate spaces of decision-making, self-esteem, and community-building. Her dissertation, "Black Girl Gaze: A Visual (Re)membering of Black Girlhood as an Act of Resistance," is a yearlong visual ethnographic account of her work with Black girls in Saving Our Lives, Hear Our Truths (SOLHOT). Central to her research is the use of documentary photography (specifically grounded within the legacy works of Carrie Mae Weems and Gordon Parks), which allows the girls to use photography as a way to document their perspectives and share those narratives with others. Building on her experiences as a youth worker, community organizer, and teacher, Taaffe is focusing her research on the integration of Black girl visual narratives into spaces of educational policy and Black/Hip Hop feminist, interdisciplinary scholarship.

Artist Biographies

Romare Bearden (1911–1988) was an African American artist and writer renowned primarily for his collages. In subject matter, Bearden's brightly colored collages featured a diverse array of topics, ranging from biblical and classical stories to jazz music and the lives of contemporary African Americans. After attending Lincoln University and Boston University, Bearden graduated from New York University with a degree in education; further study included the Art Students League of New York. Museum collections include the Metropolitan Museum of Art, Museum of Modern Art, Whitney Museum of American Art, National Gallery of Art, Philadelphia Museum of Art, Museum of Fine Arts, Boston, and The Studio Museum in Harlem. Selected publications include *A History of African American Artists: From 1792 to the Present* (1993); *Six Black Masters of American Art* (1972); and *The Painter's Mind: A Study of the Relations of Structure and Space in Painting* (1969). Among his awards are the Mayor's Award of Honor for Art and Culture in New York City (1984), and the President's National Medal of the Arts (1987).

Robert H. Colescott (1925–2009) was a painter of Afro-American life and social commentary. His work is known for its expressive figures, strong color palette, and blunt confrontation of racial and sexual themes. Under the GI Bill, Colescott received both undergraduate and graduate art degrees from the University of California, Berkeley, and began his career as an abstract painter in the Bay Area and the Pacific Northwest. A trip to Egypt in the mid-1960s inspired him to include racial themes in his work. Museum collections include the Albright-Knox Art Gallery, Buffalo; Museum of Modern Art; Corcoran Gallery of Art; San Francisco Museum of Modern Art; Museum of Fine Arts, Boston; Hirshhorn Museum and Sculpture Garden, Smithsonian Institution; and Baltimore Museum of Art. In 1997 Colscott became the first African American artist to represent the United States in a solo exhibition at the Venice Biennale.

Ellen Gallagher (b. 1965) is known for paintings, collages, and films that uncover and challenge African American stereotypes by incorporating minimalist formal concerns with pop culture ephemera, particularly postwar-era advertisements for hairstyles, wigs, and skin products targeting African-American women. Gallagher attended Oberlin College (1982–84), Studio 70 (1989), the School of the Museum of Fine Arts, Boston (1992), and the Skowhegan School of Art (1993). Museum collections include: Art Institute of Chicago; Baltimore Museum of Art; Cleveland Museum of Art; Museum of Contemporary Art, Los Angeles; Museum of Fine Arts, Boston; Museum of Modern Art; Tate Modern, London; Walker Art Center; and Whitney Museum of American Art. Gallagher participated in the Venice Biennale 2003 and in 2015. Awards include: The Joan Mitchell Fellowship (1997), the American Academy Award in Art (2000), and the Medal of Honor from the School of the Museum of Fine Arts, Boston (2001). She currently lives and works in New York and Rotterdam, The Netherlands.

In her mixed-media assemblage and installation pieces **Mildred Howard** (b. 1945) incorporates found materials and objects of personal significance into her contemporary artistic expressions, forging a link between African American folk culture and contemporary aesthetic practice. Howard received an Associate of Arts Degree and Certificate in Fashion Arts from the College of Alameda, California, and an MFA in Fiberworks from John F. Kennedy University. Museum collections include: San Francisco Museum of Modern Art; de Young Museum; Museum of Contemporary Art San Diego; Wadsworth Atheneum; Museum of Glass and Contemporary Art, Tacoma, Washington; Oakland Museum; and San Jose Museum of Art. Public commissions include: The Museum of

Glass, Tacoma; the City of Oakland; the San Francisco Arts Commission and International Airport; and the San Jose Museum of Art. Awards include: The Museum of African American Art, Los Angeles (1985); the Adeline Kent Award from the San Francisco Art Institute (1991); the Rockefeller Fellowship, Bellagio, Italy (1996 and 2007); the SPUR Award, City of San Francisco (2012); and the Lee Krasner Lifetime Artistic Achievement Award (2015).

Wangechi Mutu (b. 1972) mines the expressive possibilities of collage, assemblage, and installation to uncover and examine issues of violence toward and misrepresentation of Black women. Born in Nairobi and educated in Great Britain and the United States, Mutu brings a global perspective to her examinations of culture, representation, and social justice. Mutu studied Fine Art and Anthropology at the New School for Social Research and Parsons School of Art and Design in the 1990s, and later earned a Bachelor of Fine Art from Cooper Union (1996) and an MFA from Yale (2000). Museum collections include: Art Gallery of Ontario; New Museum of Contemporary Art, New York; Museum of Modern Art; Museum of Contemporary Art, Los Angeles; Saatchi Gallery, London; San Francisco Museum of Contemporary Art; The Studio Museum in Harlem; the Whitney Museum of American Art; and the Museum of Contemporary Art, Chicago. Awards include: Blackstar Film Festival Audience Award for favorite experimental film, Philadelphia (2013); Brooklyn Museum Artist of the Year (2013); African Diaspora Awards, New York (2011); Artist of the Year Award, Deutsche Bank, Germany (2010); Louis Comfort Tiffany Foundation Grant (2008); and the Joan Mitchell Foundation Award (2008).

In her sculptures, installations, and prints, **Alison Saar** (b. 1965) combines historically resonant materials and images that reflect the diversity of her heritage and personal experiences. Through the inclusion of references to African and Afro-Caribbean art in her work, she invokes histories and narratives that inform contemporary identities. Saar received a Bachelor of Arts from Scripps College, Claremont, California (1978) and a MFA from the Otis Art Institute, Los Angeles (1981). Museum collections include: Baltimore Art Museum; Birmingham Museum of Art; Frederick Weisman Foundation, Los Angeles; Harold Washington Library, Chicago; High Museum of Art, Atlanta; Hirshhorn Museum and Sculpture Garden, Smithsonian Institute; Los Angeles County Museum of Art; Metropolitan Museum of Art; Museum of Fine Arts, Houston; Museum of Modern Art; National Museum of African American History and Culture, Smithsonian Institution; Nelson Atkins Museum of Modern Art, Kansas City; Pennsylvania Academy of Fine Arts; The Studio Museum in Harlem; Virginia Museum of Fine Art; Walker Art Center; and Whitney Museum of American Art. Awards include: Joan Mitchell Foundation (2013); Excellence in Design Prize New York City Art Commission (2005); COLA Grant, Los Angeles (2004); Distinguished Alumna Award, Scripps College (2003); Flintridge Foundation Awards for Visual Artists (2000); Distinguished Alumnus of the Year, Otis College of Art and Design (1999); Joan Mitchell Foundation Award (1998); and the John Simon Guggenheim Memorial Foundation Fellowship (1989).

Lorna Simpson (b. 1960) began her career as a documentary photographer in the late 1970s, capturing images of daily life in the United States, Europe, and Africa. Simpson's mixed-media artistic work explores ideas of gender, race, and history, often through the reappropriation of segregation-era photographs. Simpson received a Bachelor of Arts in Photography from the School of Visual Arts (1982) and an MFA from the University of California, San Diego (1985). Museum collections include: The Art Institute of Chicago; Albright Knox Art Gallery; Baltimore Museum of Art; Bronx Museum of the Arts; Brooklyn Museum of Art; Cleveland Museum of Art; Corcoran Gallery of Art; Denver Art Museum, Fogg Art Museum, Harvard University; High Museum of Art; Los Angeles County Museum of Art; Metropolitan Museum of Art; Milwaukee Art Museum; Museum of Contemporary Art; Museum of Modern Art; National Gallery of Art, Smithsonian Institution; San Francisco Museum of Modern Art; Studio Museum of Harlem, New York; Tate Modern, London; Walker

Art Center; Whitney Museum of American Art; and Yale Art Gallery. Awards include: Artists' Space Board of Directors, New York (1989); Louis Comfort Tiffany Award (1990); Finalist, Hugo Boss Prize (1998); Solomon R. Guggenheim Foundation (1998); The Whitney Museum of American Art Award (2001); and her work was shortlisted for the Deutsche Börse Photography Prize (2014). In 1993, Simpson was the first Black American woman whose work was exhibited at the Venice Biennale.

Mickalene Thomas (b. 1971) draws from a diverse set of sources and inspirations to create her elaborate mixed-media paintings, including Harlem Renaissance artist Romare Bearden, 19th century Hudson River School landscape paintings, the color innovations of Henri Matisse, and Pop art. Using rhinestones, acrylic, and enamel to deploy her vision, Thomas challenges common definitions of femininity and beauty. Thomas studied at Southern Cross University, Australia (1998) before earning a Bachelor of Fine Arts from Pratt Institute (2000), and an MFA from Yale (2002). Museum collections include: 21st Century Museum; Akron Art Museum; Brooklyn Museum; Art Institute of Chicago; Detroit Institute of Arts; Museum of Modern Art; National Portrait Gallery, Smithsonian Institution; Rubell Family Collection; Seattle Art Museum; San Francisco Museum of Modern Art; The Studio Museum of Harlem; Taschen Collection; Whitney Museum of American Art; and Yale University. Awards include: Joan Mitchell Foundation Grant (2009); Pratt Institute Achievement Award (2009); Timerhi Award for Leadership in the Arts (2010); Asher B. Durand Award, Brooklyn Museum of Art (2012); Anonymous Was a Woman Grant (2013); Audience Award: Favorite Short, BlackStar Film Festival (2013).

Kara Walker (b. 1969) is best known for using the 19th century artistic medium of cut paper silhouettes to explore historical and contemporary issues of ethnicity, identity, and power dynamics. Her body of work also includes video and sculptures that also unflinchingly raise questions about race relations, past and present. Walker received a Bachelor of Fine Art degree from Atlanta College of Art (1991) and an MFA from the Rhode Island School of Design (1994). Museum collections include: Baltimore Art Museum; Brooklyn Museum of Art; Museum of Fine Arts, Boston; Art Institute of Chicago; Museum of Contemporary Art, Chicago; Los Angeles County Museum of Art; Museum of Modern Art; Metropolitan Museum of Art; Seattle Art Museum; Solomon R. Guggenheim Museum; Tate Gallery, London; Weisman Art Museum; and the Whitney Museum of American Art. Awards include: The John D. and Catherine T. MacArthur Foundation Achievement Award (1997); and the United States Artists Eileen Harris Norton Fellowship (2008). In 2012, Walker became a member of the American Academy of Arts and Letters.

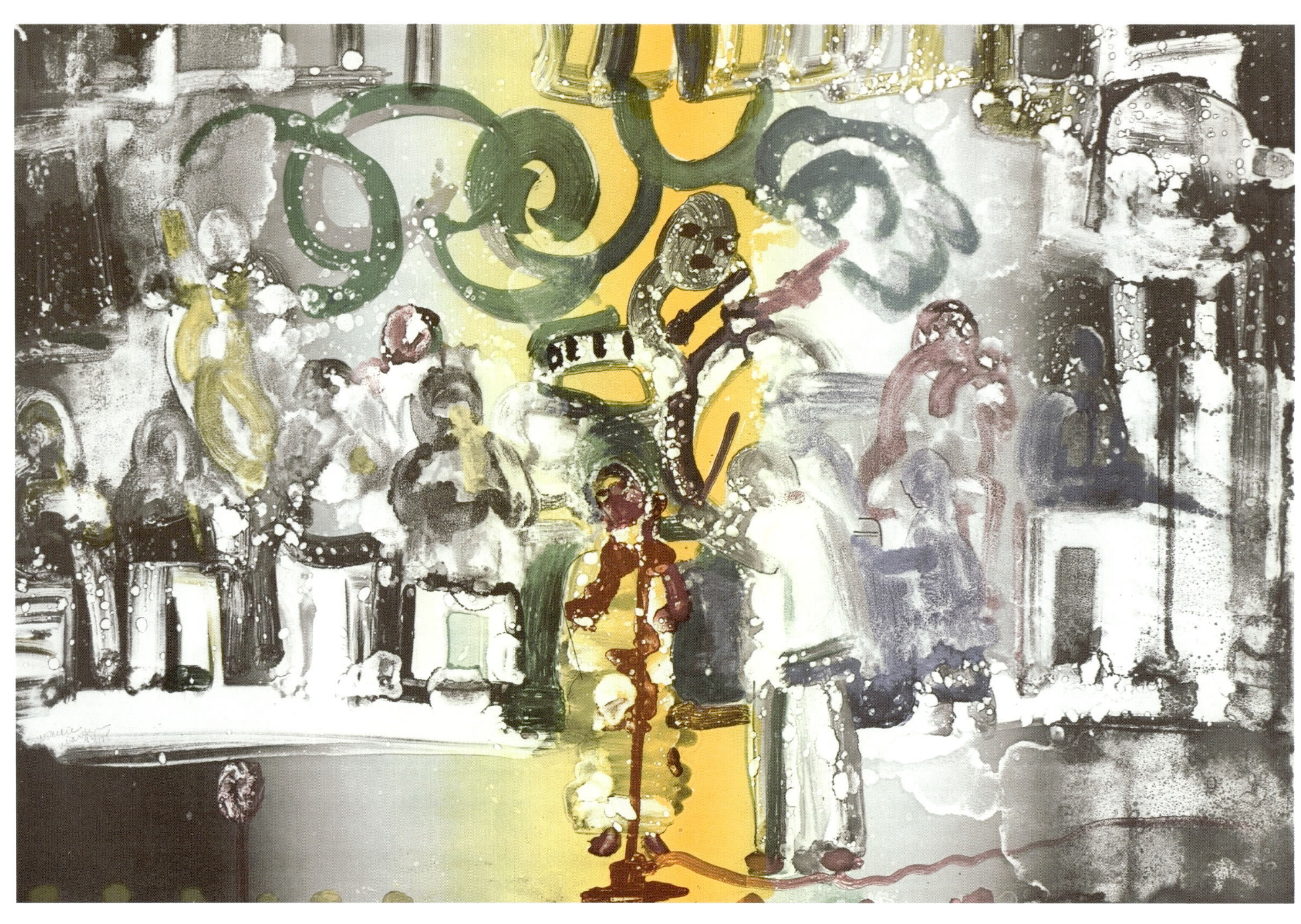

Romare Bearden (American, 1911–1988), *Jazz Series: Introduction of a Blues Queen*, 1979, lithograph, 24¾ x 34⅝ in.

Collector's Statement

WHEN I WAS APPROACHED A YEAR AGO by curator Jessica Hunter-Larsen from Colorado College about creating an exhibition that would focus on the work of African American artists I was intrigued. Coincidentally, Megan Valentine, curator of the Alexandria Museum of Art, in Alexandria, Louisiana, contacted us at about the same time with the desire to present an exhibition with a strikingly similar theme. Since we had worked with Jessica several years earlier on another exhibition called *Women's Work* in 2009, I asked if she would reach out to Megan and co-curate a show that would travel to both museums.

Both curators worked together and have created an exhibition that I think is stunning! It focuses on attitudes and opinions about how Black women in particular are perceived in our communities. The name of this exhibition is so imaginative, *Beyond Mammy, Jezebel & Sapphire: Reclaiming Images of Black Women*.

This catalogue features a number of important artists, including Romare Bearden, Robert Colescott, Ellen Gallagher, Mildred Howard, Wangechi Mutu, Alison Saar, Lorna Simpson, Michalene Thomas, and Kara Walker. While I have originated more than a hundred exhibitions at eighty museums to show work from our collection, which now exceeds more than 10,000 prints and multiples, rarely has an exhibition focused so intensely on the social and political struggles of our time by laying bare the long-held stereotypes that we find so often in our country.

The artists in this exhibition force the viewer to deal with complicated, often painful themes. They make us search inward about our values. Complementing the art in this book are essays by nationally important scholars and critics, who add another level of introspection to explain and challenge our views of ourselves.

The purpose of my collections is to help get important artists' work, like that created by the artists in this exhibition, seen in museums across our country. I feel it is critical to facilitate exhibitions so these brilliant artists can speak to each of us about the themes of our time that are important for all of us to deal with. I hope that everyone who attends these exhibitions comes away profoundly changed in a way that will help us all work together to not only respect each other, but work together so that the dream of eliminating intolerance and bigotry can be achieved.

This is an important exhibition, so please bring your children, grandchildren, nieces, nephews, neighborhood kids, whoever you can round up! As I have often said, too many eyes do not wear out the art! The only regret I might feel would be—after all the work the curators and staff at these museums have put into this exhibition—if everyone in all these communities does not get a chance to experience this exhibition!

Jordan D. Schnitzer

Published by the Jordan Schnitzer Family Foundation on the occasion of the exhibition
Beyond Mammy, Jezebel & Sapphire: Reclaiming Images of Black Women
Alexandria Museum of Art, Louisiana – December 2, 2016 to February 18, 2017
I.D.E.A. Space at Colorado College, Colorado – March 27 to May 10, 2017

FRONT COVER: **Alison Saar** (American, b. 1956), *Black Snake Blues* (detail), 1994, offset lithograph, 21¾ x 29¾ in.

FRONTISPIECE: **Robert Colescott** (American, 1925–2009), *Mother Nature (African Venus)*, 1983,
acrylic on canvas, 84 x 72 in.

BACK COVER: **Mildred Howard** (American, b. 1945), *I've Been a Witness to this Game III* (detail), 2016, color
monoprint/digital on found paper with collage, 20⅝ x 15⅛ in.

Designed by Phil Kovacevich
Editorial review by Sigrid Asmus
Printed in Canada

ISBN 978-0-692-80317-2